A Cap For The King

By
Rukshana Master

(Great-great granddaughter of Dosebai
Cowasjee Jessawalla)

Dosebai Cowasjee Jessawalla

CHAPTERS

1. The Story Begins
2. Meheribai, a bright Spark in the Darkness
3. The Spread of Women's Education
4. Dosebai's Early Life and Engagement
5. Marriage and Life with the In-Laws
6. An independent Married Life
7. Advancement and Education
8. Some more innovations in Parsi Society
9. Visit of HRH The Prince of Wales 1875
10. The Delhi Durbar and The Proclamation 1877
11. The Taj Mahal and a visit to Lucknow
12. Benares – Sacred city of India and Calcutta
13. Reception at Government House and the Marble Rocks
14. Lord Lytton at Ganesh Khind
15. On the S.S.Nizam
16. In the Capital of the British Empire 1878

17. Meeting Mrs. Gladstone and a visit to Windsor Castle
18. At the Paris Exhibition
19. Dosebai's Ascent in a Balloon
20. Meeting Mrs. Ahlers at Bonn
21. Private Audience with the Pope in Rome
22. The Ups and Downs of Life
23. Travels in South India
24. Dosebai's 2nd Voyage to England and Subsequent Tour around the World
25. Bound for Japan
26. Onwards to the USA – San Francisco to New York overland
27. Washington and the Jamestown Exhibition and England once more
28. Being Presented to Their Majesties at Windsor 1908
29. Return to India
30. Closing Reflections

CHAPTER 1

THE STORY BEGINS

Several centuries ago, India did not exist as one united country. That was to happen after many, many years, with a lot of help from a tiny island nation on the other side of the world.

There is evidence of an ancient and great civilization in the Indus valley. The 4000-year-old ruins of Mohenjo-Daro and Harappa prove this. As time went on, the fabled treasures of India attracted the Aryans, whose influence can still be seen in the people of the northern provinces. Gradually, they moved further south and integrated with the indigenous Dravidians. Around 327 B.C. Alexander the Great began a two-year campaign in Northern India. The Afghans and countless other foreign raiders, all of whom left their mark and also vastly enriched the culture of India, followed the Greeks.

By the 8th Century, there were small kingdoms all over the sub-continent, each ruled by its own royal family and each following a different religion and also speaking a different language. Needless to say, as is the way of the world, most of them fought with each other and each thought their lifestyle was the best. This feudal system was typical of almost every country in the world – the toughest and roughest being the ones who took charge and the artisans, the creative minds, craftsmen and the more gentle types taking the orders and keeping the kingdom and the royal family in the manner to which they had become accustomed.

However, now and again, a ruler emerged, who was more enlightened with a kinder and broader mind. Sometime during the 9th Century, the Kingdom of Gujerat, on the west coast of India, was ruled by such a man – Jadi Rana. One fine morning, there arrived at the shores of his kingdom, three shiploads of refugees from Persia.

They were Zoroastrians, fleeing Persia to escape persecution from the wave of Islamic fervour that threatened to destroy their way of life. They were followers of the Prophet Zoroaster, practicing a wonderfully natural science of respecting the Sun and all the elements of nature, practicing the theory of 'good thoughts, good words and good deeds', and helping one's fellowmen regardless of caste or creed. There is a lovely little story attached to their arrival in India. When they first set foot in Gujerat requesting shelter, King Jadi Rana initially refused them permission to stay, sending as his reply, a glass of milk full to the brim. This was to say 'My country is full, we have no room for you.' The leader of the people from Persia sprinkled a tiny pinch of sugar on the milk. The sugar dissolved instantly. This was his way of saying 'There are so few of us to so many of you. We can only sweeten your lives by being here.' The Hindu King was so impressed that he allowed them to stay and gave them land for cultivation and to build their homes. He also made them promise to respect Hindu customs and never to try to convert his people to their religion. They became known as Parsis (people from Pars, the Indian name for Persia). The Parsis were more concerned about losing their own identity in this hugely populated country, so they happily settled in Gujerat. Over the years, they adapted to Hindu dress and traditions, always with added finesse from their own culture. From those humble beginnings, the Parsis became leading industrialists, philanthropists and a highly respected part of Indian society.

Fast forward to the 18th Century. Parsi merchants had already established trade with the East India Company, with whose help the British were slowly but surely infiltrating India with great diplomacy and tact – making friends with one Nawab (King) and offering to help him sort out his pesky neighbour in return for minerals and other wealth. The neighbouring King would also be approached with some other deal and before they knew it, India was part of the British Empire. This is a very simplistic view, but in a nutshell, that's how it happened. One does not need an entire history lesson here, so suffice it to say that in 1858, after over a century of control by the East India Company, India was finally proclaimed part of the British Empire

2

and the British Raj was established. Which, of course, meant that most of India was English speaking for a very, very long time.

However, had it not been for King Charles II marrying Catherine of Braganza in 1662, this might have all turned out differently as Bombay belonged to the Portuguese, who gave the city (then a group of islands) its name. The islands were given to Great Britain as part of Catherine of Braganza's dowry but as Charles II did not want the trouble of looking after them, he rented Bombay to the East India Company in return for ten pounds of gold per year. Being a deep-water port and a grand trading post, it soon became a hugely successful commercial port and trade in silk, onyx, rice, tobacco and cotton flourished. In time, a fort was constructed and many stately homes for the merchants. The Parsis were the first Indian community to adopt the English language, as it was essential to trade and progress with the west. (I am confident that had it proved necessary, they would have adopted Portuguese)!

That is to say - the Parsi men were well educated, but the women, having adopted Indian customs, were not. This was all about to change in a very interesting way.

During the reign of George III in England in the late 1700s, a Parsi gentleman named Set Cursetjee Maneckjee Shroff, a wealthy and prominent philanthropist in Bombay, took a wife, Bai Barozbai. When it transpired that this lovely lady could not produce an heir, she most generously suggested that he took to himself another wife. This was done, but not without shocking the entire Parsi community. The result? Set Cursetjee was blessed with four sons and a daughter. He lived with both his wives and his many children in great happiness, until his death at eighty-one. The third son, Hormusjee, is to be instrumental in this story.

Around the same time as Set Cursetjee was causing scandal amongst the Parsi community, another grand gentleman, Set Jamsetjee Nanabhoy Guzdar, a timber merchant and also very wealthy, charitable and kind, got married and had an only child, who died at the age of fourteen. He was, naturally, heartbroken and during a trip to Surat to transact some business, he contracted a clandestine marriage (for want of a better description) and decided to return home with his new wife, much to the annoyance of the first one, but with the full approval of his mother. This second wife produced two sons and seven daughters. The eldest daughter, born in 1799, was Bai Meheribai, intelligent, beautiful and headstrong. She is also very important to this story as she married Hormusjee. This pair owed their being in each case to a second union, a coincidence that cannot fail to interest, as they became the parents of Dosebai, whose life story this is destined to be.

Bai Meheribai   mother of   Dosebai

CHAPTER 2

MEHERIBAI, A BRIGHT SPARK IN THE DARKNESS

Hormusjee and Meheribai had four sons and one daughter, Dosebai. Although brought up in an orthodox family, where a woman's place was in the home, Meheribai differed from other Parsi ladies in cultivating a wide field of acquaintances outside her own community. Possessing an independent spirit and clear sound judgment she was accustomed to taking the lead in every interesting enterprise, thus incurring the displeasure of her own circle. She was interested in business affairs and world matters, subjects quite alien to the average Parsi woman at that time.

At the age of twenty she was overwhelmed by her first grief, the death of her father. She was left a considerable sum of money in his will but as soon as it became available, her husband Hormusjee took it into his head to lay claim to it and thus the question of money, the prolific source of all evil, raised its ugly head. Meheribai reasonably suggested that the legacy should be put in trust for their children. Her husband however, would not consent to this. This led to a lawsuit being filed and much unpleasantness, which caused a great conjugal rift. Meheribai stormed off to her mother's, leaving Hormusjee to sort himself out. This step only widened the breach and Hormusjee, to stifle his feelings, launched forth upon all sorts of questionable commercial enterprises. He had full control over his father's affairs, and while speculating largely in opium on his own account, his father's business sustained a heavy loss and the burden of the entire household fell on him. His father optimistically remarked that Meheribai's legacy would be more than sufficient for them all. But worse was coming.

Her mother, in an effort to smooth things over between the couple, suggested that she agreed to her husband's demands. This,

6

Meheribai would not do, as her children would not benefit. Needless to say, they fell out over it and her mother ordered her to leave. As all she cared about was her children's future, she was abandoned by both her husband and her mother. Through the help and kindness of sympathetic friends, she was able to rent a top floor apartment, her friends supplying all the furniture and requisites. She established herself there with two sons and her daughter while two sons remained with her husband. All attempts at reconciliation proved fruitless. Hormusjee would not condescend to live in rented accommodation and she would not return to her father-in-law's house, well knowing that he had encouraged her husband's claim. Thus, two months elapsed and then, a terrible calamity broke over her head.

Separated from his wife whom he really loved and honoured Hormusjee, with no one to share his anxiety and soothe his perturbed spirit, in great desperation, took his own life. This awful intelligence reached Meheribai and in the intensity of bitter anguish, she exclaimed 'Take my all, yes, everything, but spare him'. This tragic occurrence spread horror through the entire family and drew down upon poor Meheribai the unmerciful enmity of all. Returning to her father-in-law's she passed the first days of her widowhood in deep affliction, aggravated by the hostility of those around her as in the family's eyes, this was all her fault. The only words of kindness she heard were uttered by the few friends who came to condole with her. After enduring great harshness and rough treatment from her relatives she moved, with her five children, to a separate dwelling. The unfortunate lawsuit, the prime cause of all her sufferings had, in the meantime, been brought to a settlement.

Being now relieved of money problems, Bai Meheribai, realising that this degrading treatment of women needed sorting out, turned her attention to the wants of others and extending the scope of her energy, she applied herself to the introduction of sensible reforms amongst her own people, thereby incurring the most vehement opposition on the part of the orthodox Parsis, amongst whom were the two families most closely related to herself. But her indomitable courage, her sound judgement, her inborn spirit of progress and her aspirations for the good of the country enabled her, alone and unsupported, to brave the torrent of bigoted resistance and ultimately, to sow the seeds of that culture of which we are now thankfully reaping the fruits. It is the most ruthless pruning, which produces the noblest harvest.

In 1841 she moved to a small, secluded house in Hornby Row, adjoining that of Sir Dinshawjee Manekjee Petit. On the other side stood the office of the Presidency Engineer and to the back, rose the stony rampart of the Fort, surmounted by its guns. In this new home she lived an active, happy life. Her father-in-law, Set Cursetjee, took a lively interest in her children and after the death of Hormusjee, evinced much affection towards them. But Meheribai, though rejoicing in this change, carefully maintained her control and educated her sons and daughter in conformity with her own enlightened ideas. At this time, Meheribai did what men shrank from doing and took the lead in every good innovation, extending her acquaintance to other castes and nationalities, to the consternation of her community in whose eyes she was very rash, unconventional and therefore quite reprehensible. She had no English education but was an expert in Gujerati, in which language she had a fluent and graceful style.

Through her family doctor Mr. Baptist she made the acquaintance, which ripened into friendship, of the Faria family and at their house she first met Mrs. Ward, an English schoolmistress and her mother Mrs. Mackenzie. In the companionship of these two ladies she acquired a taste for European manners and customs and her circle of English friends rapidly grew. It was then considered so completely out of order to form even an acquaintance beyond one's own caste that her conduct often provoked the remark, not unmixed with hatred, 'Is it possible for a Parsi female to enter an English house and to mix in such society?'

But, appreciating the broad and liberal principles introduced by British rule, she could afford to pass over these silly remarks in silence. To give one example, the innocent enjoyment of a morning or evening walk, to say nothing of a drive, was at that time out of the question for a Parsi female, but Meheribai was not slow to perceive the wholesome influence of air and exercise making it a rule to be out with her children enjoying the evening breeze and she had her reward in seeing them healthy and happy. But this harmless freedom was an offence to the orthodox Parsees. They, like bullocks in the mill, were content to tread in the beaten tracks of their forefathers. 'Keep the females stationary' was their motto. They were completely negligent of the wants, physical and moral, of their wives and children, though for themselves they sought every luxury and pleasure. The men-folk had their fingers in every dish from a pie to a pudding; yet they denied their wives and daughters the simple diversion of an evening ramble. The ladies of even the wealthiest families were only allowed to take the air in their own gardens, and a walk by the beach or the more lively bandstand was altogether undreamt of - that is, until Bai Meheribai set prejudice at defiance, whereupon contempt and suspicion were poured upon her by her own people, but enthusiastic applause and huge encouragement by the whole English community.

The year 1842 saw the beginning of English education amongst Indian women and it was Meheribai's bold act that enabled this. In consequence of her friendship with Mrs. Ward and other English ladies, she resolved to enter her only daughter into Mrs. Ward's English Seminary. This was at a time when fathers entertained not the remotest idea of educating their daughters. Already amongst the different people of India, Parsis, Jews, Hindus and Muslims, there was some knowledge of the English language, but that was quite one-sided. No man ever thought of disseminating it amongst the women of his community. A slight smattering of the vernacular was the extent of a young Indian lady's attainments. Indeed, here was a general desire to keep the fairer sex in ignorance.

Amid so much that was discouraging, Meheribai took the first step towards better things by introducing English education into her own family, under the benign rule of her Majesty Queen Victoria and by slow degrees, others followed her example.

Previous to 1840, what nominal education an Indian girl could receive was imparted in an antiquated and clumsy fashion. A ground floor veranda in some prominent locality, with boys and girls squatting on a hard mattress, formed the school, where the young were taught according to the whims and capabilities of their native teachers. Too often, the very appearance and habits of these male teachers – *Mehtajees* as they were called – were not such as to command respect. They sat on a mat with their grimy feet stretched out at ease, their *dhoti* (loin cloth) half drawn up and without either turban or shirt. Like the *Moolla* (Muslim priest) calling the faithful to prayer, these teachers were wont to recite at a bawling pitch of voice and in a dreamy state of sluggishness, the multiplication table, which was then caught up and repeated in a united roar by the pupils. Amid this unmeaning jargon, in such adverse surroundings, the girls of those days picked up the few crumbs of learning which fell to their lot, and even this was the portion of a lucky few, as will be apparent when one hears that only two such schools existed at the time. The native opinion was, 'Of what use is education to our females – it would not bring wealth'.

Females were, at the same time, debarred from social interaction beyond that of their own immediate circle. Thus, without education and without elevating example, they were content to run in the same channel from one generation to another. They passed the one half of their time in the routine work of the household, and the other in idleness and gossip. A noble or even useful career was undreamt of for a woman, the weaker sex being considered by the Indians vastly inferior and women's rights and wants in those days completely ignored. Hence, it can well be conceived how the action of one, and that one a woman, stirred up the wrath of the entire male portion of the whole native community, for Meheribai's independent spirit waged war upon the custom of centuries.

The man or woman who stands foremost in a reformation needs to draw strength and support mainly and mostly from an approving conscience. Meheribai had to bear the brunt of the ignorance and prejudice of her whole family and community, by placing her only daughter in Mrs. Ward's school. The school was situated in that part

10

of the Fort inhabited exclusively by Europeans, and known by the name of the English Quarter, an area scrupulously avoided by native ladies. Meheribai's young daughter going to and fro every morning with her servant created a great scandal amongst the Parsis, some of whom went so far as to send threatening letters to the family. Her own father-in-law expressed his high displeasure and all were unanimous in declaiming against the vices that English education would assuredly bring with it. In the face of this united opposition and slander, the brave mother did not falter in her pursuit of what she deemed right for her child.

Two Gujerati journals of the day, *'Jam-i-Jamshid'* and the *'Chabook'*, the former being the organ of the Parsi aristocracy – passed comments on Meheribai's conduct. Some of these Parsi lordlings had unanimously resolved to excommunicate Meheribai and her house. This news coming to her ears impelled her to write to the instigator, begging him to make his decision public. No written reply was received to this request but an emissary was sent, with a verbal message from the worthy Sethias, in which the threat of excommunication was ignored and merely their disapproval of her daughter's training expressed, thus avoiding an allegation that they could not sustain in public. Noticing this fact, the editor of the *'Chabook'*, lashed the Sethia class with the cutting taunt that 'the long beards of the menfolk have been tied up in knots by a mere woman'.It is gratifying to note that ultimately, the very Sethias who had so vigorously denounced Meheribai, came to introduce her reforms into their own families. They then prided themselves on being the champions.

After the enlistment of Meheribai's daughter into the number of Mrs. Ward's pupils, people began gradually to open their eyes to the vital importance of women's education. About this time her brother-in-law Maneckjee began to have his eldest daughter taught English by a governess. Meheribai asked her father-in-law why all sorts of objections had been raised to her daughter's education, when now his own son was allowed to follow her example. His answer was: ' It was not objectionable to have a girl taught by a lady privately, but in her (Meheribai's) case the world-wide publicity of sending her daughter to an English school was the source of objection' to which Meheribai replied in these stern words, 'Had the question not assumed a prominent aspect in the public newspapers, Mr. Maneckjee would not even have thought of the same and I trust as you, my noble benefactor, have seen your son in this instance following my footsteps, so you will, God willing, see many other reforms introduced among the Parsees through my instrumentality'.

From all these facts it is evident that the widow lady, Meheribai, was the first to sow the seeds of education and emancipation amongst Indian women. In those days, however great or enterprising a project might have been, its author never courted popularity through the medium of the public press, as is often the case nowadays, when every trifling incident is trumpeted forth and rendered unduly weighty. On account of the old-fashioned suppression of women's achievements, it is no wonder that Meheribai's name did not appear at the head of the much-lauded supporters of female education, and that the generations succeeding have not done her ample justice.

Mrs. Ward's English School ceased to exist in 1847, when she returned to England. However, Dosebai's English education continued under an English Governess. She went on to achieve astonishing and unusual things, including travelling around the world and meeting the British royal family. She was also my great-great grandmother. In her dotage, she wrote a wonderful book, with the highly original title of 'The Story of my Life', which was published by the Times Press, in Bombay in 1911. Read on!

CHAPTER 3

THE SPREAD OF WOMEN'S EDUCATION

The preceding pages bear witness to the important part played by Meheribai in laying the foundation of women's education in India. Her example, through its value, was emulated in due course by other Parsi parents and publicists. The Jews appear to have been the first to follow the Parsis in this respect, and all honour is due to Sir Albert Sassoon, for bringing the means of education to the women of his creed. He lived near Meheribai and soon a close friendship sprang up between the two families. What Meheribai did for the Parsis, Sir Albert succeeded in doing far more fully and effectively for the Jews. He overcame the prejudices of his traditional education and spread the light of many a beneficent principle, opening the gate of happiness to the women of his faith. Jewish women, according to Dosebai, never appeared in public without closely veiled faces. When the ladies of the Sassoon family came to visit Meheribai, they would never unveil till the male members of the household, servants included, had removed themselves and the coast was clear; but sometimes, their fancied security was invaded, by a visit from Dr. Fogarti, the family doctor, who would call unannounced, unaware of the presence of strangers. All hell would break loose as they attempted to hide themselves in adjoining rooms – causing much merriment. Happily, thanks to the good sense and energy of Sir Albert Sassoon, this custom of veiling was dispensed with.

Meheribai's contacts outside her own community did not cease here. She was equally friendly with the two wives of an eminent Hindu, Set Khimchund Moteechund, both of whom were equally desirous of emulating her Parsi dress and elegance. They took to wearing English dresses or Chinese silk saris, as well as Parsi-fashioned *Lahe* saris, and enjoyed the luxury of slippers, after the manner of the Parsis. As Hindus, they formerly went barefoot. *Lahe* was an intricate, minute and laborious process of embroidery. The stitches, the size of a pin's head, were made from a pattern on raw silk fabric, which, then being dyed, made the tiny specks stand out in relief on the uniformly coloured ground. The artisans who produced this frequently required a whole year to finish a piece of the length of six yards by one. This form of needlework is now almost obsolete on account of its great expense and ostentatious appearance.

In 1846, an Englishman, by the name of Mr. Hinton established a school for Parsi boys, which was supported by the leading gentlemen of the community. Subsequently in 1849, Mrs. Hinton opened a similar school exclusively for girls and enrolled several young ladies of the Sassoon family amongst its pupils. By the thorough course of instruction pursued in these schools, the results could be compared favourably with those of English institutions.

The Marathas were next to adopt English education for women after the Parsees and the Jews, and subsequently the Hindus and Mahomedans. The Bethune Female School at Calcutta came into existence in 1848. About 1849-50 the Parsis of Bombay established a female school for vernacular education only. Its existence was made possible by generous donations from Messrs. Patel, Cursetjee and Camaji and other wealthy Parsi gentlemen, who thus won for themselves the reputation of being promoters of female education. But we must not forget that one courageous woman made the first step towards this. With regret we note the fact that this girls' school was founded seven long years after the commencement of female education, and those who gave it the mere assistance of their purse were held up to the admiration of the world, while the real founders of education by moral support were either forgotten or ignored.

Finally seeing the benefits in educating women, if only to have an intelligent conversation with one's wife, in the year 1860, Dosebai's uncle, Mr. Manekji Cursetjee Shroff, opened, at his own expense and at his own residence in Byculla (a suburb of Bombay), a school for girls, which after some time was, with the financial assistance of a few friends, transferred to a suitable building in the Fort and publicly opened under the name of 'The Alexandra Native Girls' English Institute'. The school was open to girls of all castes and creeds.

Under the influence of Queen Victoria's reign, the education of Indian women flourished. Some aspired to excellence in the fine arts and others even ventured to appear in print. Every facility was now afforded to the pursuit of study. Time had, to a great extent, overcome the conservatism of the Parsis, whom we now saw in the vanguard of progress.

But let us revert to the events in the life of the lady who thus laid the real foundation of women's education in India. During her widowhood, about the year 1848, Meheribai moved to the exclusive suburb of Malabar Hill, a step that occasioned as much outcry as sending her daughter to school had done. The Parsi Panchayat, the body conducting the social governance of the Parsi community, gave it out as their grave opinion that it was anomalous for a Parsi lady to live in such an out-of-the-way locality. The newspapers were equally busy in discussing the point, some defending, others opposing Meheribai, all of which only had the effect of encouraging her in the prosecution of what she deemed best and most suitable. At the time, the healthy eminence of Malabar Hill was quite untenanted by any Parsis. Most of the lovely bungalows in this beautiful and green locality were owned or rented by Europeans.

On the 9th April 1879, in the eightieth year of her age, Bai Meheribai breathed her last, up to which time she had been in full enjoyment of health of body and vigour of mind. In an editorial article published in 1908, the *Indian Magazine and Review* of London paid this fitting tribute to her memory: '*Meheribai Shroff distinguished herself by those qualities of which heroines are made. She realised the advantages of giving an English education to Parsi girls long before other women and even most men of her race. But, building ideals is one thing, and translating them into action quite another. For this reason, her name deserves a prominent place in the history of women's education in India*'.

15

CHAPTER 4

DOSEBAI'S EARLY LIFE AND ENGAGEMENT

When Dosebai became an adult, at the grand age of fourteen, she was obliged to discard the childish dress, alike in girls and boys, of short, brightly coloured trousers, jacket and cap and adopt the 'Sari' – a piece of cloth six yards in length by one and a half in width, sufficient to wrap around the whole body and cover the head. As an adult, she also had to give up wearing boots, and take to slippers instead, a change that she thought no improvement at all, but custom forbade a grown-up Parsi lady to put her feet into anything else. She was only thirteen when she left school, but every Saturday she drove over to the Fort and passed the day in the agreeable company of her old school friends. She continued her study of English at home, under the tuition of a governess, who came twice a week for half a day to teach and converse with her. By keeping up with her English friendships, she acquired many English manners and customs which were very different from those of Indians, and her mind became insensibly tinged with English ideas, so that she viewed life differently in many respects, from those around her.

A Parsi lady of the time would not have considered it disrespectful or odd to squat on the floor in company, talk in a loud tone while gesticulating freely, stare at others and the like. Dosebai's English mistress inculcated habits of gentleness, respect, order, tidiness and politeness, and taught her to obey and also respect her own religion. She took delight in observing her precepts, which made her honoured and beloved both at school and at home. When she was present at any Parsi festivity, her manner of sitting appeared to the others, affected, and she was requested, in terms by no means flattering, to sit at ease as they did and stop putting on airs and graces. When she spoke, her modulated voice was considered pretended coyness. But those who then condemned her behaviour, gradually began to view with exulting pride the repetition of it in their own daughters or grand-daughters and she often heard a grandma announce, her wrinkled face lit up with joy, that Soonabai goes to school or that Aimai and Shirinbai are learning English. Parsi parents were suddenly most eager to give their daughters every means of improvement. To her, nothing could be more gratifying than this complete reversal of feeling in the question of female education.

When a marriage was about to take place in a Parsi family, invitations were issued to between two and five hundred friends and the festivities extended over a period from five to seven days. This used to entail a great deal of unnecessary labour for the ladies of the household. Letters of invitation were sent only to the gentlemen, after which a priest visited each one, requesting the honour of his presence on the morning of the Wedding Day. But in those days, the method of inviting the lady guests was most tiresome and nonsensical. The principal ladies of the host's house were obliged to go round amongst relatives and friends, two days before and again on the morning of the wedding day, to proffer and reiterate their invitation and not until they were nearly prostrate with fatigue, would the guests consent to come – such was the perverted notion of politeness. To make an end of this most stupid and trying custom, her mother, on the occasion of the marriage of one of her brothers, sent cards of invitation to ladies as well as gentlemen. The greater number responded to her invitation, but others held aloof at the innovation. Their house not being large enough to accommodate so many guests, her mother was allowed the use of the adjoining Engineer's office, an arrangement that was quite unaccountable to the Parsis, who began to think there was no end to the wonderful things her mother could do.

After the wedding festivities were over, Dosebai and her mother retired for a time to Malabar Hill where they lived in a tent, until a small bungalow that her mother had in course of construction, was completed. They were the first Parsis to settle in Malabar Hill. In time, they made the acquaintance of their European neighbours, who were as astonished at their arrival as if they had come from another land. (Could this have been the origin of the word 'hill-billies)?

While living at Malabar Hill, Dosebai and her youngest brother contracted cholera, and as no medical assistance was to be had in those days in that remote locality, they were removed to their house in the Fort where, by the timely assistance of the family physician, they recovered. Had it been otherwise, people would not have been slow in laying the blame on their distant abode. In the treatment of this terrible disease, the doctor had strictly warned them not to drink water but, being unable to endure their intense thirst, they contrived to elude the vigilance of their attendants and drank copiously of some water that had been left standing in the empty room for two months. It was a complete miracle that they both survived.

However, the heaviest storm follows the most unruffled calm. In 1849, her youngest brother, who had escaped the malignant seizure of cholera, died of a slight attack of fever. This was an irreparable loss to their now limited domestic circle and her mother's health gave way completely under the burden of grief. It was at this time and under these unavoidable circumstances that Dosebai took a sorrowful farewell of her studies, at the age of seventeen. The care of her invalid mother and the domestic duties of the house now devolved upon her. After a death in the family, the Zoroastrian religion required that, for a year, the survivors observed numerous ceremonies for the departed spirit. Different foodstuffs had to be prepared every day for the deceased, and every month, on the date of death, a special ceremony was held, for which many sorts of sweetmeats were requisite, over which the priests recited appropriate prayers. This was called 'Baj'. It was necessary, on these occasions, to treat fifteen or twenty priests to dinner. (Needless to say, as in most religions, the priests made up the rules). In these observances, for the express benefit of the departed, rich and poor gave willingly and generously, glad to have their opportunity of showing their regard for the dead. (Not that the dead had anywhere to spend it). All the food had to be prepared under the direct supervision of the ladies of the family and in strict accordance with the rules laid down by the religion. It fell to Dosebai to supervise the preparation of these offerings to the memory of a beloved brother and with a full heart she entered into the melancholy duty, and soon became a very good cook.

She became adept in the making of sweets and soup for her mother, who could not at first be brought to believe that what she so much relished was the work of her daughter's hands. Even in the quiet retirement of mourning and sick nursing, her liberal education stood her in good stead, for with keen zest and enjoyment she performed the household duties that others felt to be drudgery.

The year 1850 was an auspicious and momentous one for Dosebai, as she was then pledged to a partner for life. Up to this date, early marriages, or rather infant marriages, were the universal rule. It was no uncommon sight to see a baby at its mother's breast pronounced, by the priest, a married person. Twelve years was the maximum for a girl to marry. If, through untoward circumstances, a daughter remained unmarried at the age of fifteen, it was a grave sorrow to the parents, and the girl herself became the butt of cruel taunts while scandal was busy with her name. Setting all the force of her character against this pernicious custom, her mother would not hear of marriage for Dosebai till she had reached her sixteenth year. Marriages were then entirely arranged by the parents, the young people having neither voice nor cognizance of it till all was settled. Thanks to her association with English ladies, Dosebai had come to the conviction that she had the right to either assent or decline any proposed union; that she too, had something to say in a matter of such grave importance to herself.

Before his untimely demise, her father had destined for Dosebai his brother's son, and such a connection would not have been distasteful to her, but on account of her mother's separation from the family, she was not sure how the case stood. She was much in favour with her uncle, the father of the boy, and from her childhood, she had been invited to his house every week, as well as on her birthday, where she spent the day in much enjoyment with her cousins. This could not fail to please her, and so impressed was she with her uncle's kindness that she constantly exclaimed to her friends – 'What a lovely uncle I have! He gives such grand entertainments on my birthday!' She discovered, much later, that her birthday was also the anniversary of her grandmother's death, and that the festivities were in honour of the dearly departed, though her uncle killed two birds with one stone by making her believe that she was the heroine of the day. On these occasions, she would converse and associate freely with her cousin, but their long-contemplated union was, according to Parsi custom, never broached between them.

One day, acting under her mother's advice, she asked her uncle to make her his daughter-in-law, according to the express wish of her father, but he answered that, though he loved her as his own child, he could not, on account of his objection to her mother, consent to her union with his son. From this, she understood plainly that only if her revered and beloved mother were no more could she aspire to be the wife of her cousin. Her mother therefore, sought a match for Dosebai elsewhere. (Her descendants will be forever grateful as there are enough eccentrics in the family already). Here, may be mentioned another custom, which thwarted the happiness of many a couple. As soon as a child was born, the parents had its horoscope prepared by a Hindu astrologer, and when, therefore, a marriage was in contemplation, the first step was to produce the two children's horoscopes, submit them to the opinion of competent astrologers and either proceed with the proposed match or give it up, according to the verdict of these authorities. This idle superstition made many an ill-assorted marriage and also, marred many an auspicious one.

After her brother's death, at which time Dosebai was seventeen years of age, they received numerous visits of condolence from their relatives and friends. Amongst the number was a cousin of her mother – a rich, elderly widower. He avowed to her mother his affection towards Dosebai, offering to make over to her all his wealth and property, if she would become his wife. This was tempting bait to her mother, who believed her daughter's happiness would be secured by this generous proposal. Dosebai, however, thought otherwise, but dared not say so, as it would have been held in the highest degree undutiful and unprecedented to decline an offer already accepted by a parent. In her distress, she turned to Bai Baiai

Jessawalla, her mother's most intimate friend, and with tears streaming down her cheeks, she confessed to her the repugnance she felt for the contemplated union. Baiai lovingly consoled her, by promising to use her best efforts to dissuade her mother from carrying out her intention, and fortunately, her endeavours were successful for she never heard another word of this ridiculous idea.

CHAPTER 5

MARRIAGE AND LIFE WITH THE IN-LAWS

Only a month after this happy release, an incident occurred which served to prove the secret workings of Providence in the events of human life. Her mother's friend Baiai, had the sudden misfortune to lose her young and beloved daughter-in-law, who was cut off in the prime of life and happiness leaving six children and a young husband to mourn her untimely loss. This sad event plunged the whole circle into profound grief. They were a large and united family, all living together in love and harmony in the parental homestead. In consequence of the mourning in both families, there was a cessation in the daily visits Bai Baiai paid them, and Dosebai as an unmarried girl, could not go out alone, the custom being that after a death, a full year must elapse before the relatives may pay even their closest friends a visit.

Her hugely practical mother had a brilliant idea. It was that her friend might make Dosebai her daughter-in-law. Very soon, a rumour arose that Dosebai's mother had betrothed her to the widowed son of her friend. Subsequently, Baiai came over and all preliminaries were discussed and arranged between her and Meheribai. The only objection was the charge of six motherless children, which she considered too great a burden for her daughter, but on being assured that the paternal and maternal grandmothers would share the care of these little ones and that they would be provided for, she was relieved and all anxiety was set at rest. Mercifully, Dosebai declared that of her own free will, she chose this friend's household as her future home and selected Baiai's son as her future partner for life. Parsi ladies who had attained the dignity of grandmotherhood, always cherished and took care of their grandchildren during the remainder of their lives, thus helping and relieving the parents to a very great extent. In those days, there used to be no contact with the opposite sex outside the immediate family circle. Thus, her mother, though on intimate terms with Bai Baiai, had never seen any of the male portion of the family and Dosebai naturally, had not even seen, much less talked, to him who was now her affianced husband.

In the weak state of Meheribai's health, she thought it advisable to hasten the betrothal and she did so by sending, according to Parsi tradition, the following items to the bridegroom: a diamond ring, a bouquet of flowers, a packet of sugar candy, 'kunkoo' (red powder applied on the forehead), some pure silver fishes (wrought by Chinese workmen), betel nuts and leaves, both real and in silver. All of these things were sent enclosed in a copper box, instead of on the usual tray, so as not to hurt the feelings of the late wife's parents who lived in the house with the bridegroom's family. It was considered quite unusual to think of a second marriage for at least one year after the death of one so young as the first wife.

A few days after this, her future mother-in-law sent her in return, costly suits of silk, and so the betrothal was ratified and soon became public knowledge. In those days, the Parsis did not allow an engaged couple to meet or correspond with each other from the betrothal until the marriage tie proclaimed them one. So during this interval her intended husband went on a tour to inspect his father's branch establishments in Upper India and the Punjab. These were situated in Karachi, Sukkur, Mooltan, Rawalpindi, Kabul and several other places. In those days, before railways and posts were known, travelling was hard and tedious. Her fiancé, Cowasji Jessawalla, who had been in the habit of making such journeys from the age of seventeen, went from Bombay to Karachi in a small sailing ship and from there, up-country on horseback or camelback returning to Bombay for two or three months in the summer. It was quite unthinkable for a son to follow a different business calling from that of his father, and each son vied with the other in maintaining the prestige of the paternal house as handed down from one generation to another.

It was in the year 1850 that her fiancé started on his tour, returning two years later. The date for the wedding was set for 30th

May 1852. During the long engagement, no correspondence passed between them, though she ardently longed to see him, or at least, to hear how life was faring with him. From his mother, she received assurances of his unchanged love for her and with that she had to be content, but her English friends found it quite incomprehensible that she could endure such a long and silent engagement. Her fiancé's friend, Mr. Arthur Lynch, teased her for having chosen a husband without having seen him, and who, for aught she knew, was neither comely nor handsome, to which she answered, 'It is not so much the body as the mind we love, and seeing that my betrothed is highly spoken of by everybody, my mother thinks she gives me into good hands, and I myself expect to be happy.'

The long-awaited marriage was celebrated in traditional style, but the fact of this being a second marriage on the bridegroom's part called for a moderated expression of rejoicing. Although the festival was kept as unostentatious as possible, Dosebai's mother lavished upon her only daughter all that the fondest love could suggest. All their friends were duly invited, but on her husband's side only his two sisters, his sister-in-law and her mother-in-law's cousin were present. The ladies dressed her in a beautiful white sari, put the red mark of *kunkoo* on her forehead, garlanded her head with flowers and accompanied her onto the flower-bedecked stage where the marriage ceremony took place, according to Parsi custom, at 7 pm.

After this, the young couple were escorted to Cowasji's father's bungalow at Tardeo, where his family had taken up residence two days before to prepare for the reception. It was not customary for the young couple to walk together, so the bridegroom headed the male part of the procession and the bride followed with the ladies. Thus, she reached the bungalow, where she was heartily welcomed by her new relations. Her husband continued on his way to the family residence in the Fort, where she followed the next evening.

Before crossing the threshold of Dosebai's future home, flowers, rose petals and raw rice were scattered over her head. A coconut and an egg were circled over her head three times, and then smashed on the ground, respective symbols for good luck and fertility. This

24

ceremony was known by the name of '*Achoo-Michoo*'. From that day, she became a member of the large family, consisting of between fifty to sixty persons, all living under one roof. (What a thought)! Needless to say – it was a huge and spacious mansion they lived in. Some of the presents that her mother gave to her husband on the occasion of the marriage may be mentioned as an example of what was usual in Parsi marriages of the time.

She presented every member of his family, male and female, with handsome suits of silk and sent shawls and turbans to the managers and clerks of his firm. On each intervening holiday during the first year, she gave Cowasji a suit, a costly shawl and a diamond ring, at the same time bestowing gifts on each of his children by his first wife. To Dosibai, she gave all sorts of culinary utensils such as pots, crockery, trays and large copper vessels, ornaments of silver such as coconuts, dates, betel nuts and leaves – a suite of carved black wood furniture, a valuable bedstead with silken hangings and coverlets – a cow and a nanny-goat – sewing materials in rich abundance, a work table, a writing desk and a large sum of money. Thus her loving mother gave expression to the joy she felt at seeing her only daughter united to such a good and exemplary man.

From the year 1852, down to the time her partner departed this life, the course of Dosebai's life was a happy and easy one, blessed with the unceasing love of her husband and the pleasant intimacy of a large family circle. All the female members of the family were very old-fashioned in their ideas and way of living, but nothing was wanting on her fond husband's part to ensure her comfort, indeed, love prompted him to anticipate her every wish. Thus, on the first day of her new life, he handed her the keys of a cupboard in which she found all manner of things perfectly suited to her taste. There were silk stockings, silken fabrics, kid gloves, pieces of lace and tulle, velvets, bottles of attar of roses, handkerchiefs and every requisite of sewing and writing. It was a delightful surprise, as she certainly never expected to see such luxuries in a house where old customs prevailed, but her husband's liking for English fashions agreed with hers. She asked Cowasji whether his former wife had also been of the same mind and he smilingly replied that she had been 'of simplicity itself'. He further went on to say, ' My family is a large one and quite of the old school. You, however, blessed with an English education as well as being trained in Parsi usages, will wisely discern how to maintain family concord without depriving yourself of anything to which, from infancy, you have been accustomed.'

Her endeavours brought their own reward in the good feeling shown to her by her numerous relatives, though no doubt, the new customs she introduced sometimes annoyed them. Her fond mother had accustomed her from childhood to dress carefully and in good taste, both at home and abroad, and now that she was under the authority of her parents-in-law, she continued the same habit, dressing as a young and happy wife, in bright, silken stuffs at home and bedecked with diamond and pearl jewellery when at parties and entertainments. The only ornament in general use, amongst the ladies of her husband's family, were the ear and nose rings, while their housedress was simple in the extreme. To wear costly outfits when at home was then comparatively unknown. Her mother-in-law, whom she affectionately called 'Auntie', supervised Dosebai's meals herself and looked after her every comfort in detail. Within the family the old fashioned style of eating together while squatting on a low couch prevailed, the luxury of table, chair and place settings being unknown. Her indulgent mother-in-law, foreseeing that it would be difficult for her to take part in such meals, provided for her exclusive use plates, cups and tumblers, besides serving her meals in a separate room and often providing a extra dish or two for her benefit, secretly however, to avoid kindling envy.

When at home, her husband would join in the repast, which, though now a common custom, was then unprecedented, as males and females in those days ate apart. To Dosebai, it was a source of great pleasure to see how his views ran in unison with hers, and owing to her being with child at the time, the affectionate solicitude of her two mothers and husband was redoubled. In her joy, her mother presented her with a set of splendid diamond and pearl ornaments and her husband's parents gave her some in gold, in addition to which, every holiday her husband laid a sum of money

26

before her, telling her to spend it on ornaments of her own taste and design but, as she had jewels enough, these sums remained in her hands and accumulated.

In readiness for the birth she removed to her mother's house, where she was, in due course, safely delivered of a daughter. The baby received the name of 'Goolbai', the choice of name always resting with the child's grandmothers. Forty days after confinement she wished to return to her husband's house but to this her mother was most averse, desiring her to stay with her till the child had completed her fifth month, which was another daft old tradition. To this Dosebai would not consent, and her mother was cross with her, saying that if she persisted in going away, she would give no presents to the child, and also take back the ornaments she had given Dosebai on her marriage. Her fond husband, on his daily visits, soon realised that something was amiss, and on her acquainting him with the matter, he calmed her down by telling her to provide everything for herself and child at his own expense, and that they would go home at the appointed time.

As was the custom, she prepared an ornate costume for her mother-in-law, garments for her infant, large tapestry coverlets for taking the child from one place to another, toys, cups and saucers, plates and milk jug all of silver, a tray full of sugar candy, a basket of wheat, a cradle with netted curtains and a cot. 'All this', she said to her mother, ' I have to thank you for', with which polite fiction, her mother was somewhat mollified. However, when she set out for her husband's house, accompanied by a nurse carrying the baby and her husband's sisters, who had come to take her home, her mother did not relent, which made Dosebai unhappy, as she was reluctantly compelled to appear with the few simple ornaments she had received from her husband. All this material bargaining was the order of the day. Thank goodness times have changed!

As already mentioned, she introduced some new fashions into her husband's family, including the use of stockings – Parsis of the old school never wore them. (Why anyone would want to wear stockings in a tropical climate is anyone's guess). As she had been accustomed to wearing them all her life, it would have been impossible to give

27

them up entirely. She had always kept them on in her own room, but taken them off when mingling with the family, but now her husband's express wish was that she should wear them always and go in them everywhere. Her sisters-in-law saw with displeasure her husband's growing inclination for new ways, but as time wore on and his love increased, his ideas ran more and more in the same channel as hers, inspiring her with confidence and making her independent of his sisters.

In 1854 on the occasion of a second pregnancy, Dosebai, happily accepting her husband's wishes, remained at home, under the tender care of his mother, but the baby did not survive its birth. Her mother was most annoyed that she had not gone to her. Cowasji's family began to regard Dosebai with dislike, because her husband was in the habit of lavishing money on her. Whatever she did or her husband gave her seemed to augment their jealousy. But the love of her husband and his worthy mother towards her was not lessened one iota.

Cowasji was the chief executive of the family firm, and was invariably consulted on all matters, commercial and domestic. He was too busy during the day to be able to join in any leisure activities, with very few exceptions. He devoted any spare time to his aged parents, whose love for him was truly touching. Through his unwearied exertions, the prosperity of the firm considerably increased and his father's confidence in him was so great that the direction was left almost entirely in his hands. Shopping in a high street being, in those days, unknown, the men in the family made all purchases from pedlars and artisans plying the streets, the women and children wearing, without comment, whatever they were given.

Hindus and Parsis dressed pretty much alike in bright red, green or yellow fabrics, the tailor's taste being unquestioned, and his ugly, badly sewn garments were the universal mode. After Dosebai's arrival amongst her husband's relations, her sister-in-law, the wife of the other son, felt it awkward to accompany her in walks and visits, as her clothing was not as sophisticated as Dosebai's. So, with the kind permission of her father and mother-in-law, she had some

28

dresses and ornaments made, similar to Dosebai's, but even in this trifling business she had no voice. Dosebai, however, thanks to her sensible husband, and possibly her bossy nature, was at full liberty to dress as she pleased.

Three years after the marriage, Cowasji's only brother fell dangerously ill. It was customary in cases of illness, before resorting to medical aid, to consult the invalid's horoscope, and a handful of wheat was passed over his head, from which a Brahmin astrologer pretended to prognosticate whether he would recover or not. To serve their malicious purposes, her sisters-in-law made their mother believe that the grains of wheat had plainly manifested that her son's illness was caused by Dosebai – the new daughter-in-law. Her kind mother-in-law would not at first credit this assertion, but it did alienate her affection for Dosebai, whose third confinement was impending. Unaware of the gathering storm, she resolved to remain, for the approaching event, in the family house, but her mother-in-law, hitherto kind and considerate, did not condescend to ask her wishes and intentions, and this most unaccountable silence seemed to her like hail in harvest. She pleaded with her husband to have the mystery cleared up by going direct to his mother and asking her the cause of her dissatisfaction, but he, who was kind to a fault, would rather bear injustice than take anyone to task. (He was probably terrified of his mother). So, he advised Dosebai to let things take their course and said that if his mother insisted on being awkward, they would move to the bungalow in Tardeo.

Eventually, her husband resolved to ask his father's permission to go, temporarily, with her to the Tardeo bungalow. He feared however, that the expense and luxury of a separate establishment would be considered unseemly for a lengthened time and that his father would be opposed to such a plan. But, as Dosebai knew enough of the management of a house and liked the idea of having a home for herself, her husband and her children. For, although she had tried from the very day of her marriage, to conform to the antiquated habits and notions of her relatives, the result had been failure and disappointment. On the 1st February 1855, they left the family residence for a place of their own.

Dosebai taking the reins of her Phaeton Carriage and horses.

CHAPTER 6

AN INDEPENDENT MARRIED LIFE

The bungalow in Tardeo had only one storey and was furnished very simply, but as for air and sanitation, was greatly superior to the family mansion. Here, Dosebai passed the first day of her independent married life with delight, and here was to be her future home and the birthplace of her succeeding children. She and Cowasji made it a rule to dine together with their children at one table every evening. Not only was it the custom to eat apart, but also driving together, except in a closed carriage with the panels and venetian blinds closely shut, was undreamt of. No Indian lady had ever been known to drive in a phaeton or any other open carriage. The luxury and benefit of living, as a small family unit, in a bungalow, was also comparatively unknown.

Of course their change of residence gave rise to ill-natured remarks, but on the other hand, it added to their enjoyments, chief among which was the pleasure of having their own garden. They did not go to the length of taking a drive together, as the in-laws would definitely not have approved of such a step, and although Cowasji was unconcerned about public opinion, he was always obedient to the will of his parents. In spite of great coolness on the part of her mother-in-law, Dosebai paid her a visit every few days. Of the six children by her husband's former wife, four remained at the family house and two accompanied her to the new home. Surrounded with domestic comfort and with good and efficient servants, her life now became a very happy one.

With servants to look after the children and do the housekeeping, and with none of our modern distractions, Dosebai became a brilliant needlewoman, embroidering, amongst other things, an entire sari of white satin. There were flowers, fruit and other beautiful designs all over in intricately decorative stitches. She wore this sari on the occasion of her sister-in-law's wedding and it was much admired.

She even produced a heavily embroidered palanquin rug, as a present for their friend Colonel Jarvis, who had it shipped to his stately home in England. Many years later, she was to present two of her exquisitely embroidered pieces to their Majesties King Edward VII and Queen Alexandra.

Her English friends were astonished at the work on the sari and asked her how she had the patience to go through such an amount of labour, as one yard of such fine stitching would have been quite enough to wear them out. Besides this, she embroidered various outfits for children, sari borders, numerous caps, boots and slippers, some for use in her own family, and some as presents for her friends. Such hand made things, though not of much value, were most acceptable and prized far above their intrinsic worth. In return, they sent her presents of their portraits, writing or sewing materials. The interchange of such inexpensive presents was quite an innovation, as up to this time, the cost of a present had been its only criterion of worth with a Parsi and anything, which did not represent a high figure, was unacceptable.

Another irksome and ridiculous mode of gratifying one's friends and relations was that of sending trays full of sweetmeats on the monthly and also annual ceremony for the dead. These sweetmeats were very troublesome to prepare, and therefore, the first recipient would discharge her obligation to another friend, by sending them on to her, she in her turn would despatch them to another and so on, the original tray full of sweets sent off early in the morning would be seen knocking about from door to door, till even considerably past midday. Dosebai's Parsi friends, contrary to her pleas not to do so, insisted on sending these questionable benefits to her far-distant bungalow at Tardeo. As the tray-load consisted of a variety of foods over which the priest had performed prayers, only Parsis could partake of them. As they reached them at a late hour and were considerably past their best, they could not even give them to the servants, and therefore they went, usually, to fill the belly of a cow or other domestic animal. To avoid all this waste and possibly safeguard the health of domestic animals, Dosebai ultimately made it a rule to decline, with thanks, such presents, although at the risk of offending the donor. It was gratifying, however, to note the steady decline of such stupid customs, as also of other ceremonies for the dead, entailing heavy expenditure and much waste of time.

Another custom, which she would have liked to have seen abolished, was that of sending large quantities of cakes and fruits at Christmas, to Europeans. These were sent only in the name of the husband, who wasted large sums upon them. These expensive presents, coming all at one time, served no other purpose but to be handed over to the servants, for the Europeans themselves, though receiving them on the one hand, on the other only laughed at the absurdity. It might be reasonably asked why Europeans did not return the compliment paid them by sending to Parsis at *Jamshedi Navroz* (New Year), or to Hindus at *Divali*, something of the same kind, instead of ignoring these occasions, which were of as much importance to Indians as Christmas was to them. Her husband and father-in-law formed no exception to this rule and she could not dissuade them from it. Since however, she was blessed with independence, she did away with these expensive follies and substituted self-made keepsakes, which she liked both to give and to receive. Surely such a gift, trifling though it might be in value should be more acceptable, than expensive and useless articles, only given to preserve a silly custom.

After the birth this time, of a still-born child, her health was much impaired, so for her personal comfort and convenience, her husband gave her a carriage, in which she could enjoy the luxury of an evening drive. Before this, she had seldom stirred out for an evening walk or drive, but generally spent these cooler hours with her children at home, or in sorting out the servant situation. After the acquisition of the carriage, she began to frequent the bandstand, where she was the only Parsi lady to be seen. In those days this salubrious resort had no attraction for them, their one idea of enjoyment being comprehended in visiting and gossip, when the inexhaustible topic of discussion was the ceaseless feuding of mother and daughter-in-law, or the sorcery used by some wife to make her husband a slave to her will, and inflict on her mother-in-law an incurable malady, or how Soonabai, though past sixteen was still unmarried, and Bachoobai waits for her betrothal in feverish anxiety, and Roopabai would not condescend to call her daughter-in-law, and that Dinabai's daughter would not go to her new home. (Today this would make the story line for a TV soap).

In some families, for the ten days after a death had occurred, from two to four hundred females congregated daily, ostensibly to condole with the bereaved. It can readily be imagined how tales were then carried, from one ear to another, and that they lost nothing in the telling. This, and the practice of questioning servants, who casually called at the house with messages, as to the habits and doings of their mistresses, were the two prime sources of mischief making and tale-bearing. The steady growth of education, bringing with it wider interests and occupations for the mind, was a great improvement, indeed.

Life at Tardeo awakened in her and the children a love and taste for gardening, in which mornings and evenings were delightfully spent and the year seemed as if it had been but a month.

In 1859, when anticipating her fifth confinement, she was urged by the Doctor to curtail her household duties and to rest as much as possible. She therefore availed herself of this time of enforced idleness, to renew her study of English. In the month of July she was delivered of a son, who received from his grandfather the name of Dadabhoy, after a very jovial and bulky friend. Eleven days after the child's birth, her estranged mother-in-law appeared, in company with this gentleman, Dadabhoy Framjee Divecha, who carried a tray filled with clothing, caps, toys and sweetmeats for his name-child.

Here is another strange custom, which used to be observed by young Parsi mothers. For the first three days the child may not be taken from the mother's arms, for five days the mother desisted from all wheat based food and for ten days from all animal food, eggs included. Then a ceremony, called the 'Ten days *Gote*', was gone through, after which she could eat what she liked. Dosebai threw off this tyrant yoke of superstition and subsequently the whole family did the same. This '*Gote*' ceremony was evidently borrowed from the Hindus and like many other customs, is still practiced in some Parsi households.

Also in the year 1859, her husband retired from his father's firm and secured the post of guaranteed broker to Messrs. Volkart Brothers, a flourishing German firm established in Bombay. His honest and straightforward dealings commanded the esteem of his employers and contributed to the popularity of the firm. Mr. George Volkart had great respect for Cowasji's business acumen. A year later, Cowasji fell ill of malignant fever, and on medical advice was moved to a friend's bungalow at Malabar Hill. Here, Mr. Volkart was their next-door neighbour and called regularly twice a day, to enquire after the patient. Sometimes he would drop in about 8 pm and chat with them sitting beside Dosebai on the sofa, much to the disapproval of her mother-in-law and other aged relatives who, after he had gone, would expostulate with her on the monstrous impropriety of which she had been guilty. But these friendly visits were very agreeable to her. In those days not only would a Parsi lady not sit in the same room with a European gentleman or converse with him, but if she saw him coming along the road she would escape up some by-lane or into the nearest house. The sight of an English soldier or civilian on the steps of a house would throw its female inmates into hysterics or send them flying like frightened rabbits, whilst the servants hurried to shut the doors, to the great discomfiture of the stranger who could not guess that he, himself, was the cause of all this confusion. The Parsi ladies could not speak or understand a word of English, nor often, of Hindustani, and as the servants could not command enough courage to ask or answer a question, they excused themselves by saying they feared that the females would all swoon away in fright. But instead of blaming the domestics, this nonsensical timidity had to be attributed to the opponents of women's education, who restricted the acquaintance of their wives and daughters to the limited circle of their nearest relatives.

Her husband, under the judicious treatment of Doctors Sylvester and Miller, was soon restored to health. They celebrated his recovery and the first birthday of their son, Dadabhoy, simultaneously with friends and relatives flocking to them with their congratulations. Cowasji now resumed his official duties, and all was back to normal.

In 1860 Dosebai resolved to visit Poona in company with her stepchildren and other relatives, to the number of about thirty. None of the party had ever made such a journey before. Poona, roughly 120 miles from Bombay, was a hill station much favoured by the British for its temperate climate. Although she had enjoyed more freedom than any of her Parsi sisters, she had never been further than a couple of hours drive from Bombay. The Parsi population of Poona then consisted only of traders, and it was rare for the luxury of this cool retreat to be enjoyed by any of the Bombay community. They set out on their journey early one morning in October, and after taking a short halt for lunch at Khapolee, at the foot of the Bhore Ghat, they continued on their way up and over the Ghats in horse-drawn hackney coaches. (Ghats are tortuously winding mountain roads). These fairly unstable vehicles jolted pitilessly, now sinking into a deep rut, then perching on a high mound, but they were a merry party and these ups and downs only added to their fun. At 6pm they reached her father-in-law's bungalow at Khandalla, some 50 miles from Bombay. After a restful two days at this pretty place, they continued on the bumpy and dusty road to Poona.

Reaching Poona, once the renowned capital of the Peshwas and a city of unparalleled historical importance in the Deccan, at 6 pm, it presented a most unique and interesting appearance in the evening twilight. A good friend had kindly placed his bungalow in Bhowanipeth at their disposal, and here they were made very comfortable.

They took long drives and rambles on foot in the city. Among the most interesting sights in Poona may be mentioned the Temple of Parvati, in classical white marble atop a hill and the waterfall at the Bund gardens. There was a beautiful public garden known as Hirabagh, with shady avenues and green lawns, in which stood a palace called Ainabagh built by one of the Peshwa's prime ministers. The Peshwas were the original rulers of this part of India. During their visit, which took place at the end of the monsoon, it drizzled often and the city and its neighbourhood looked fresh and inviting. Their spirits recharged, they returned to Bombay by the same method and probably needed another holiday to recuperate from the journey.

Just to give a little idea of the wealth and luxury some of the Parsi families enjoyed, thanks to their association and trade with the East India Company and other countries, here is an account of a burglary that took place at Dosebai's house in Bombay.

One night in November, during the new moon, an incident occurred which mystified them exceedingly. On this evening, Dosebai had gone, with her friend Manekbai, wife of Sir Byramjee Jeejeebhoy, to see the *Divali* illuminations, from which she returned at about 11pm. Two hours or so after she had retired to rest she awoke, thinking someone was in the room, but seeing no-one, she concluded that the children's ayah had slipped in to look after her charge and soon, she was lost in sleep again. Early in the morning one of their gardeners woke them with the tidings that many trunks and boxes were lying exposed in the compound. She then saw her sewing case lying on the floor of the bedroom, furniture misplaced, and trunks missing from their places. At that time, ornaments to the value of from two to three lakhs of rupees (£20,000) were in her possession, and in the pocket of her husband's coat there was a bundle of cash amounting to 30,000 rupees (£2000). Every one of the Chinese boxes and cabinets had been opened and ransacked. One of these, full of English silks, had been eased of its contents, which were scattered all over the room showing that each fold of every piece had been searched. On the table lay, amongst other things, caps embroidered in pearls and lockets containing watches, none of which were abstracted or even disturbed. In the compound they found similarly, that the boxes had been wrenched open and their contents thrown aside after minute examination; a curious heterogeneous display of gold embroidered clothes, silver knives and forks broken and twisted, pieces of China silk all unfolded and mingling with the dust, leaves and dew of the garden. But of all this, nothing, not so much as a needle, was missing. Her jewels, evidently, had been the object of the thief's search and nothing less would satisfy him, but by a lucky coincidence they were safe in an unlikely receptacle, quite beneath the notice of their would-be possessor, and the cash was still in the pocket of the coat hanging upon a peg.

As it was usual to put on every available item of jewellery during the *Divali* holidays, she had put all hers ready for use into an old cupboard, not even locking them up, and so their insecurity was the means of saving them. As nothing had been stolen, the police could not trace the bold culprit. That it must have been someone well acquainted with the interior of the house was plain, for he had evaded the night watchman attached to every big private house, had entered through the veranda and open doors (it being midsummer), and searched in exactly those places where she would normally deposit her jewels. Her suspicions fastened upon a cook they had recently dismissed and she believed he was in collusion with the Portuguese ayah. The former, although an excellent cook and a hardworking servant, had frequently incurred her displeasure for his audacious and unceremonious conduct in entering her private apartments unannounced, in spite of repeated instructions to ring the bell before doing so. His defence was, that in none of the other Parsi families where he had served, had he ever seen a bell, which made him forget his instructions.

Soon after, their little son Cursetjee died at the age of two years, and in the same year they lost a sincere and beloved friend with the sudden death of Mr. George Volkart, just four days before his intended departure for England. When Dosebai went to condole with his lonely widow, Mrs. Volkart told her that a week before her husband's death, she dreamt that she was travelling home to Europe with her brother-in-law and her husband was not with them. Sadly, she saw this dream realised, for within a week she started for England with Mr. Pearson.

The new Manager, young Mr. Ahlers, was very kind and polite to Cowasji. Every morning Cowasji took him along to the Cotton Green, where he was taught the rules of cotton selection. They soon became good friends. It greatly pleased and interested him to see Dosebai so unlike other Indian ladies, mixing freely in English society. Soon after his arrival, Mr. Ahlers being Consul for Holland, entertained a party of Dutch travellers who were making a tour of India to observe the manners and customs of the inhabitants and the capabilities of the country. As Mr. Ahlers wished to show his friends a Parsi family at home, Dosebai invited them to luncheon one day and also invited a large party of English and Indian officials, as well as several Parsi ladies and gentlemen, to meet them.

In those days no Parsi would eat in the presence of foreigners, nor appear at a table where prohibited food (beef and pork) was served, as it was on this occasion. Their Dutch guests were therefore surprised when their host and hostess did not share the repast with them, and were much interested in the explanation that she gave them of the religious prejudices against certain articles of food. (The restriction against beef was due to the promise made by the Parsis, when they arrived in India more than six hundred years earlier, to respect the sacred Hindu cow and the restriction on pork was simply because it was not advisable to eat pork in hot countries, as it could kill you if it went off. This was perfectly logical and nothing whatsoever to do with religion, really). The host was a mere spectator at the feast or at most, served his guests with wine and pledged their health, but nothing further. Note: there was absolutely no restriction on wine.

The luncheon over, Dosebai led this 'gallant little troupe' as Mr Ahlers called his Dutch guests, to the houses of several of her relatives and friends and to the residence of a *Bania*. The travellers found all these houses tasteful and sumptuous beyond their expectations. They were especially surprised to find that a *Bania* (Hindu merchant) lived in such comfort and luxury as they saw in the house of Set Kalliandas Manmohandas. He and his wife, Kesarbai, were the first of their community to adopt the style of living of the English. Similar to Dosebai's, their bungalow was tastefully furnished, a gatekeeper patrolled in front of the house, the hall was magnificently decorated and their European friends also found, to their amazement, the comfort and refinement in this Hindu abode was equal to, if not better than, most European homes. The Dutchmen, on seeing the superb bedroom, asked Dosebai if the bedstead was kept for use or only for show – a silly question, which made her laugh at their conceit. When Europeans saw, with their own eyes, how incorrect their surmises were about Indians; Dosebai smugly noticed that their supercilious superiority was taken down a peg. The travellers were quite amazed to learn that the faultlessly appointed carriage and pair, which took them from place to place, belonged to none other than her *Bania* friends. After these gentlemen had taken their leave, she received a letter from Mrs. Ahlers, expressing thanks for the hospitality shown to her and her Dutch friends, not omitting to convey in the same letter, the expression of the very favourable opinion entertained by her friends about Dosebai, herself.

Dosebai in hand embroidered saree

CHAPTER 7

ADVANCEMENT AND EDUCATION

Here, we might mention one of Dosebai's closest friends, Kesarbai, in whose character was blended the most admirable traits of her sex and the noblest influences of Hinduism. A sisterly affection existed between them. It was a unique sight when the two of them went out together, a Hindu lady and a Parsi lady in one carriage, attired exactly alike in sari, choli (blouse), and slippers. Kesarbai even acquired the habit of putting on stockings, and had all her ornaments fashioned after Dosebai's style. It would have been impossible to distinguish the difference but for the white kerchief worn on the head by Parsi females. Kesarbai's own caste ridiculed her for having become a 'fashionable Parsi lady'. Their friendship drew forth much comment, and they were respectively designated 'Dosebai's Kesarbai' and Kesarbai's Dosebai', but nothing cooled their attachment, and a separation of a week was enough to create uneasiness in either mind. Her disposition was sweet and child-like. Their short friendship of eight years was, sadly, brought to a close by the untimely death of Kesarbai in 1869.

In 1863 Mr Ahlers and Cowasji wished to go to Surat (in Gujerat, on the west coast of India, north of Bombay) on business. They proposed that Dosebai should accompany them for the benefit of a little change of air. When Parsi families went on an excursion, they needed a week to prepare and then carry along with them a host of children, with ayahs and servants. She was told about the excursion one evening and the following morning saw her fairly equipped for the journey – the children were left behind, under the care of her step-sons and their wives.

At that time, there was no railway from Bombay to Surat, but the *SS Taptee*, of which Cowasji was the owner, plied between the ports so they accordingly embarked upon it. The party consisted of Mr.

Ahlers, Mr. Johnson, Cowasji and his wife. The weather was calm and the conversation was animated and interesting, Mr. Johnson being elderly, and Mr. Ahlers witty and of a jovial disposition. There were other Parsi women on board whose remarks reached Dosebai's ears. 'See, see,' they whispered, 'the female yonder sits and walks in the company of Europeans' (or words to that effect). Arrived at Surat, she and her husband stayed at the house of their friend, Mr. Antee, while the other two gentlemen went to the traveller's bungalow. They found the town dull, with no interesting features to engage a traveller's attention and smothered by dust, which found its way into their eyes and even their mouths while talking. It appears that Surat was not the restful sanatorium it was supposed to be. They left, after a stay of four days, but on the way back were doomed to serious trouble. Going to the steamer in a small boat, the wind suddenly began to blow a hurricane and the waters threatened to engulf them. The little boat was tossed on the waves like a plaything. The crew were thrown into a state of fright and consternation and could not discern the '*Taptee*'. Thus they drifted about, in the dark and stormy seas from 6pm until 4am; their lives were despaired of and they themselves, encountering no boat or other means of rescue, gave themselves up for lost. As for Dosebai, she could scarcely give utterance to a word, so frightened was she, but she tried to fix her thoughts upon Him, the Protector of all mankind.

Ultimately, at 4 am the storm abated, and they could perceive the lights of the steamboats and within half an hour, they were safely on board. Alarmed at their prolonged absence in such a tempest, search boats had been put out, but none had crossed their path. They reached Bombay the next day, full of gratitude to Almighty God for their miraculous escape from a watery grave.

Around this time, Dosebai began to order out from England silks, textiles and ornaments and, privately, set up a little commercial enterprise. In addition to this, she turned her attention to the care and management of horses. Every morning, she made it a rule to go to the stables and supervise the grooming and feeding of their horses, treating them to slices of bread from her own hands. This would fully occupy her for a couple of hours, much to the annoyance of the

43

grooms. After her round of the stables, she devoted another hour to culinary matters, teaching the servants how to cook various dishes to Parsi taste and instructing them in matters of cleanliness and order. Then she would go to her room and repeat the necessary daily prayers, after which she set to her needlework, patterns for which she transcribed, with such alterations and additions as her taste suggested, from English and Parisian fashion-plates. She never made extravagant use of her money at milliners' shops, like many English ladies, but purchased raw materials, from which she made curious and artistic garments for herself and for others. Even this elicited unpleasant remarks from some Parsi ladies. Confident, however, that soon hundreds would imitate and adopt her fashions, she did not care a smidgeon for what the ignorant said about her.

In 1862, Cowasji's business partner wished to send a competent man to examine the accounts of the business with the firm's branch in England. This fact reaching Dosebai's ears, she earnestly requested her husband to recommend her brother, Dorabjee, who was very clever at accounts. This was, to her delight, acceded to. To her, his employment for nine months in a princely city of the western world was highly satisfactory. She, therefore, left no stone unturned to further his felicity and prosperity. Her other brother, Heerjeebhoy, saw himself, through her husband's influence with Mr. Stevens, the senior partner of Sir Charles Forbes and Company, installed in that office.

But, happiness can be as transitory as the rays of the evening sun. Time, in its ceaseless course, often spreads woe where prosperity has reigned supreme. The year 1866 was at once the most propitious and the most disastrous known in Bombay – the mania for speculation raised many a one to the pinnacle of opulence, only to whirl him down to poverty undreamt of. A black cloud of adversity suddenly obscured the bright sun of prosperity and the wealthy upper class made huge losses and faced bankruptcy, whereas the hoi-poloi took advantage of the Insolvent Act and whitewashed themselves clear of all liabilities, pocketing whatever they could lay their hands upon. The general credit thus being shaken, those who would have been able in time to pull through their difficulties were compelled to take advantage of an Act, known as the 28th, specially framed to meet the emergency of this panic.

Cowasji had, in partnership with unprincipled persons, become seriously involved, and his entire personal wealth was swallowed up in the general chaos. The friendly support of the office officials was their only comfort in this terrible crisis. Several banks stopped payment, the credit of native merchants was gone and hardly one in a thousand escaped the universal ruin and stigma of insolvency. The Europeans concerned in these failures made their way home as best they could, and thus the once smiling Bombay fell into the grasp of the fell fiend – despair. Dosebai, however, did not give way to despondency, but gathering courage and patience from reverse of fortune, willingly gave back all the jewels showered on her by her fond husband in happier days. These proving unequal to their heavy liabilities, a mortgage on the family estate became inevitable. Kind Mr. Ahlers came at this juncture to their aid by furnishing them with a very large loan and continuing her husband's interest in the firm intact. From this time, she took the domestic economy entirely into her own hands, parted with some of their carriages and horses and, as occasion required, made use of a sum of money which she had earned through her commercial enterprise.

On the strength of her father-in-law's signature, the bank had honoured several drafts payable on sight; at the time when they fell due, payment was demanded. This threw her father-in-law and husband into a dilemma from which they could not extricate themselves, so in the nick of time, she came forward and parted with all her personal jewels, realizing a large sum to the intense relief of father and son, who overwhelmed her with expressions of eulogy and gratitude. It was during these troublesome times that Cowasji's younger and only brother died; his aged father took this sad bereavement much to heart and they all participated in his sorrow.

At this time, an affliction of the chest from which Dosebai had long been suffering, assumed an acute and dangerous character. All other remedial measures having been proved abortive, the physicians recommended as a last resource her being taken to sea, and it was decided that she should make a sojourn on board her husband's steamboat, the '*Taptee*', but her debility was such as to preclude all possibility of transit. It seemed that she was in the last stages of consumption and she was weary of life when at last, a cure was found. Her mother's family physician, Dr. Yule, was brought to see her. He gave her a number of tiny, white pills (which we now know to have been homeopathic medicine), ordering her to take a certain number three times a day, to live entirely upon milk and to confine herself to her room. By these means a marvellous improvement was brought within the short space of a week. The doctor gradually allowed her to revert to her ordinary diet and mode of living and within a month, she had regained her health. From this it will be seen that a change from one pharmacopoeia to another sometimes does good.

Previous to Dr. Yule's visit, when her case was pronounced hopeless, her daughter's father-in-law had telegraphed to his son, in London, to send his wife home to Bombay to take a last leave of her mother. Very soon Goolbai was by her side. Seeing her mother so far restored, she concluded that the danger had been exaggerated, and the presence of her dearly loved first-born soon dispelled any lingering disease. Her daughter had given birth to a son in London, the child was only nine months old and had been left in the care of his father and a nurse.

After a stay of around two months, Goolbai took her departure and they all escorted her on board the steamer to see her off. Her journey to and from England alone and unattended, and while still in her teens, furnished a topic of interesting gossip.

In those days a Parsi lady would not go in a carriage from Mazagaon to the Fort unaccompanied by her mother, elder sister or at least an ayah, and it was seldom that Parsi females stirred out, without several clubbing together to countenance and protect each other. Her daughter's courage, therefore, gave rise to snide remarks, but she couldn't give a toss as she was terribly confident. Her Hindu friend, Kesarbai, wittily versified this incident. Her rhyme may be translated thus: 'Amongst Parsees, one Meheribai gave birth to a daughter named Dosebai, in whom reforms doubled. She in turn gave birth to a daughter named Goolbai, who thinks it is not too much to go and come alone from England, and this trebles the reforms. When Goolbai brings forth a daughter, all social reforms will have gained their extreme ends, and then all Parsis, orthodox and reformed, will agree'. As it happened, Goolbai had a son, but his wife followed in the tradition of feisty females in the family. More about her, later!

The work of adding a storey to the bungalow, which had been kept in abeyance on account of their monetary losses, was now resumed and completed, all expenses being defrayed from Dosebai's private funds. In the course of this work, she actively supervised the same and in a measure acted as foreman, in which novel capacity she spent most of her time, no doubt to the great bemusement and irritation of the workers.

At the close of December 1868, they went to Nassik, to pass the Christmas vacation there. Reaching the station at midnight, they could not find transport, so they slept in the waiting room. After a few hours, while the queen of night still held full sway, they started in a *tonga* (horse and cart) and a pair of mules and reached the city at the break of day. It was then the depth of winter, and the cold was more intense than they had ever experienced before and they imagined that it was like this in England. The presence of her beloved husband gave much pleasure to the excursion. The city of Nassik was very ancient, and considered sacred by the Hindus. Being situated on the River Godavery, the climate was very pleasant, as was evinced by the keen appetite they developed there. Being then heavily pregnant again, and in a delicate state of health, Dosebai had to return sooner than had been intended.

Subsequently, in March, she gave birth to a daughter. She was named Baiai after her mother-in-law. During the forty days seclusion, which was like solitary confinement (another ridiculous Parsi custom), she could not see any of her European friends, except those ladies with whom she was on intimate terms, and whose curiosity prompted them to come and see the strict observance of the rules of her religion. Mrs Ahlers and Mrs Baker (wife of Colonel

Baker, Under Secretary to Government in the Public Works department) were her closest friends and they frequently visited and conversed with her. During previous occasions of this nature, Mrs George Volkart had paid similar friendly visits. To them, it seemed incredible how anyone could voluntarily pass such a long time in a comfortless, prisonlike place and they would ask her how she, who loved English freedom, could have the patience to comply with such a tiresome and senseless custom and why she did not set it aside, as she had done with other old Parsi customs. To this she replied that, though she liked to deck herself out in English array and though she had advocated many salutary reforms, it by no means followed that she would deviate from any rule laid down by her religion; no matter how much discomfort the observance entailed.

The year 1870 was a memorable one for India, for it marked the visit of an illustrious guest, HRH the Duke of Edinburgh (Alfred, second son and fourth child of Queen Victoria). The news of his advent was hailed with delight by Her Majesty's loyal subjects and fitting arrangements, for the reception for the first time of one of her children, were at once set on foot. Government resolutions were issued requesting the people to whitewash their houses, observe cleanliness throughout the city and make a suitable display, all which they cheerfully did as they were eager to impress the Sailor-Prince. Accordingly, after visiting other cities, His Royal Highness came to Bombay, where an august assemblage of Feudatory Chiefs and Princes had gathered to pay their respects to the Queen's son. On this occasion, Parsi women, casting off their awkward reserve, were seen threading the streets and entering into the spirit of the day and Dosebai, who had, for a while, taken leave of gaiety, returned to it now with fresh zest. She first saw His Royal Highness from the balcony of a Hindu temple near Byculla Bridge, as the royal procession was passing along Parel Road and again, when he was going to visit an Indian prince, the Thakore of Bhownagar, who had taken up temporary residence in a bungalow adjoining theirs. On this occasion, she and several other Indian ladies stationed themselves at the gates of their compounds. Presently, the carriage of His Royal Highness and the Governor of Bombay came along. On seeing them, Sir Seymour Fitzgerald saluted. His Royal Highness, with courtesy, raised his hat and returned their salaams, while she fervently invoked benedictions on him and his gracious Mother.

After this joyous event, Dosebai received the welcome tidings that her daughter and her husband would shortly come back from England and settle in Bombay. Goolbai and her little son arrived first, and according to her father-in-law's instructions took up her quarters with her in-laws, where after two months, she gave birth to a daughter. The poor girl was made to conform to the Parsi system and spend forty days in retirement, which at her previous confinement in London she had failed to do. The child was given the name of Rattanbai, after her paternal grandmother. Soon after this, Dosebai's son-in-law Dadabhoy, reached Bombay.

Dosebai's pleasures were now entirely of a domestic character, for having within a comparatively short period, undergone eleven childbirths, her health precluded her from taking long journeys and for the same reason, coupled with her husband's exceedingly retiring disposition, she gradually left off going to the large entertainments of Government House and elsewhere; in fact, she had ceased to hanker after such gaieties. (She was only in her late thirties)! When it became known that a ball was to be given at Government House, everyone desirous of being invited went there and registered his name, and invitations were then sent to those whom the Government thought fit. Up to the fourteenth year of her life, she had been a constant guest at these parties to which she went in the company of her grandfather. Later on, she never ventured alone into such an assemblage and it was but seldom that she went with her husband. Now, in the companionship of her daughter and son-in-law, her chief relaxation was an evening drive.

After having lived six liberated years in England, they found it irksome to be cooped up from morning till night in the parental home, so they spent every third or fourth day at Dosebai's house, when she was careful to have everything prepared for them as they liked best. Every week or two she gave a small party for her son-in-law and a few of his friends who had been to England to finish their education. Like a dutiful son, he was ever obedient to his father's will in living under his roof and dining everyday with him, so being thus dependent he could not invite any of his friends to his father's home. Therefore, Dosebai sought to please him, by entertaining them at her house. With a mother's pride she delighted to bedeck her daughter with dresses and jewels, exactly the same as she wore herself. Being of identical height, they were generally taken for sisters. A friend, Sir Frank Souter, often made the absurd mistake of addressing Dosebai as Mrs. Cama, and her daughter as Mrs Jessawalla, declaring it was impossible to make out who was the daughter and who the mother.

One morning, a picnic was planned at the caves of Elephanta, off the coast of Bombay. The party consisted of their relatives and the young friends who met periodically at her house. They set sail before the peep of dawn – a merry party - with the servants preceding them so that everything was thought of to make their enjoyment complete. However, ere the day was over, every one of them was chilled to the heart by the dread that the finale to their picnic might have to be played out in the law courts of Thana, 20 miles distant from Bombay, for, in the exuberance of youthful spirits, her cousin, Jehangir, said something in fun to a stranger; this person resented the liberty and would have dragged them all before the Thana Judge, if the more sedate members of their company had not known how to pacify him. (It is highly likely that some money changed hands). With somewhat subdued feelings they reached home safely at 7 pm.

Amid such days of gladness, the gloom of bereavement again broke in. In June 1871, she lost her beloved daughter Baiai, after one day's illness from diphtheria; she was just two and a half years old but so healthy and precocious as to have been always taken for twice her age. This equally sad and sudden blow plunged her into inexpressible grief, and she could only derive consolation from a belief in the immutable will of an all-ruling Providence and the instability of earthly joys. As an antidote to her grief, her husband took her for a change of air to Sewree, her daughter Goolbai and her children keeping her company. The love of her dear little granddaughter, Rattanbai, did much to cheer her up. Her son-in-law and cousin used to visit them frequently, and in their ready-witted and jovial company she, in a measure, 'steeped her sorrows in forgetfulness'. On account of its airy and pleasant situation, Sewree was now and then resorted to by pleasure-seekers, but it had no permanent residents. Every variety of the freshest fish, such as was very seldom to be had in Bombay, was available here. There were two or three bungalows for the occupation of Customs House officials and also a large cemetery for the Christian population of Bombay, where Dosebai used to go in the evening stillness. The general aspect of this small suburb was refreshing and calming. After a stay of a month and a half, they returned to Tardeo.

In October of the same year – 1871- the small coterie of friends made a short sojourn at Matheran, another of the delightful hill stations around Bombay. They took the morning train and after lunch at Neral Station, completed the remainder of the journey up the mountain by road, Goolbai and the other young people riding on ponies, and the older ones being accommodated on palanquins. The climb was very steep (in the modern day, the train takes on a second engine at Neral to push it up the hill).

They reached their destination at 6 pm and took up residence in the bungalow known as 'Arnold Lodge', which was placed at their disposal by the Hon'ble Framjee Patell. They refreshed themselves with 'the cup that cheers without inebriating' (I think that means tea) and soon forgot the fatigues of the journey. At supper, Dosebai pledged the health of all her comrades (with the proper stuff this time) and offered hearty thanksgiving to God for having restored her daughter to her side. Many of their friends were at Matheran at this time and there was great interchange of hospitalities amongst them. Dinner was invariably served up on some moonlit terrace where, under the serene canopy of heaven, with the clean air of the surrounding valleys and mountains playing around them they all met together and spent the last hours of the day in harmony and joy. A trip to Matheran is now common enough, but in 1865 only a couple of Parsee families had been there. To her great regret, her kind husband could not be with them on this occasion due to business commitments. After a stay of six or seven weeks they returned to Bombay, young and old, all much invigorated by the mountain air.

51

Shortly after this, she heard the happy news of an approaching marriage in the family of Sir Byramjee Jeejeebhoy and she promptly set about inventing some new sort of fancy work for the occasion. Devoting much time and thought to the task, she at length commenced an entirely original design for a cap to be worn by her son at the approaching festivities. The basis of the cap was black velvet, upon which eighteen coloured miniatures of the family were to be arranged; each tiny picture was set in a golden rim with thin glass over it (as the face of a watch is covered with glass fixed in a ring), each profusely surrounded with small pearls set in gold embroidery. In the centre of the crown came her husband's likeness, with his seven sons ranged around him and her father-in-law's portrait was placed in front, on the rim of the cap. Beside this she placed her own likeness with the pictures of her daughter and her grandchildren filling the remaining spaces. It took her two months to complete this unique picture-gallery.

It is hard to imagine that Dosebai already had grandchildren while still giving birth to her own children.

As she was in mourning for her little daughter, she could not take part in the pre-nuptial entertainments, though there was no objection to her daughter and the other children doing so. Her sister-in-law came in person to entreat her to put off her mourning for the time and go to the festival, so on the marriage day itself she went in a plain evening dress. The gathering that day at Set Byramjee's house was impressive. The Governor of Bombay Sir Seymour Fitzgerald, with his entire entourage, was present with many of the leading Europeans of Bombay. Her friend Lady Sassoon, with her daughter, Mrs. Gubbay, was also there. They saw Goolbai for the first time since her return from England and a warm friendship sprang up between the two daughters. The cap was by this time, the focus of attraction; her son who was wearing it was positively fatigued by the innumerable calls upon him to satisfy the curiosity it excited amongst the large and brilliant company that had assembled to celebrate the nuptials. Three days later, she received the following note written on behalf of her father-in-law,

'*Respected Bai Dosebai,*

Hearing from Set Dadabhoy Hormusji Cama of the elaborate workmanship of a cap embellished with our family photographs, which was worn by your son Jamsetjee on the occasion of the wedding at Set Byramjee's, grandfather desires to have a look at the same. We shall be glad if you will kindly bring it with you when you come in the evening.

Faithfully yours, Rustomjee Jamsetjee Pesikaka'

Frequent visits from all and sundry testified to the widespread interest produced by this unique fancy work. It was assiduously copied, although the services of men versed in delicate handiwork had to be found to reproduce it. Women of that time, remember, did not use their skills commercially.

CHAPTER 8

SOME MORE INNOVATIONS IN PARSI SOCIETY

On the 4th April 1872, Sir Albert and Lady Sassoon held a splendid ball for Sir Seymour Fitzgerald, the then Governor of Bombay, to which Dosebai and her daughter were invited. The only other Parsi ladies present were the two daughters of Judge Maneckjee, who from their early years had accompanied their father wherever he went. Before this, no Parsi ladies were known to have attended a ball, but on this occasion her daughter was the first Parsi woman who joined in the ballroom dancing, which constituted a novelty in the eyes of both Indians and Europeans. The fact was widely commented upon in the English and native journals, the former of which were all in favour of the movement and gave them their hearty congratulations. Some of the native newspapers, however, vehemently condemned the innovation and sarcastically criticised her daughter's conduct, while private individuals lodged complaints with Dosebai's father-in-law, characterising her conduct as scandalous and indecent. Her aged relative at first regretted these proceedings, but on her explaining to him the merits of English society, he quite agreed and said, 'Nothing but rank envy could put such a dubious interpretation upon such an innocent pleasure'.

Eight days later, when they were on their way to another ball at Government House they heard, from the mounted policemen who were stationed at short intervals along the road, the dreadful news of the assassination of Lord Mayo, the Governor-General. The eager guests turned round and made their way back home with heavy hearts. Indeed, the entire populace felt genuine horror and sympathy as soon as the tragic event became known.

It may be worth inserting here, a strange prediction of this appalling event. Invitations to the Ball having been issued four days previous to the date of the entertainment, Dosebai was busily engaged in preparing a dress suitable for the occasion when their friends assembled as usual at her house. One of them said in jest, 'There are still four days to go to the ball, why are you working so hard? If someone were to die in the meantime, all your trouble would be for nought!' To which comment, another gave this melancholy response 'The death of any of us could not prevent the ball, but that of the Governor or the Viceroy, would'. The fulfilment, alas, of this statement, happened four days later, and they were not a little bewildered that the sad prophecy of a sudden fatality should be so exactly verified.

Lord Mayo was a hugely important international diplomat and perhaps, the third most powerful person in the British Empire after Queen Victoria and the Prime Minister. On 8th February that year he stopped off to admire the view in the Andaman Islands, a British penal colony in between India and Burma. Indian convicts were then sent to the Andaman Islands and a thoroughly dissatisfied Pathan convict from the Northwest frontier, stabbed him to death. Although this caused chaos amongst diplomatic circles, it was decided to play the incident down, as there was already a lot of unrest in Asia against British rule, and this news would have been fuel to the fire. Which is probably why the news did not break in Bombay until April.

In November, (1872), the new Governor-General of India, Lord Northbrook was expected in Bombay and a grand Durbar was to be held at which the native Princes and Chiefs were requested to be present. Magnificent tents were erected on the Esplanade for the occasion and Bombay was spruced up. Besides the Rajahs, some influential natives were honoured by invitations from Government. Cowasji, Dosebai, Goolbai and Dadabhoy were present along with six other Parsis. All the Princes and Chiefs heartily responding to this invitation were there, bearing precious presents. The Begum (Queen) of Bhopal was also amongst them, but veiled. By command of Queen Victoria, the Begum was invested with the order of G.C.S.I. (Knight Grand Commander of the Order of the Star of India) by the Viceroy.

On the 19th November, Sir Albert and Lady Sassoon gave a splendid ball in honour of Lord Northbrook. Amongst the guests were to be seen representatives of several sections of the native communities. Nevertheless, there were, again, no other native ladies present save Dosebai and her daughter. The English, who assured them that if they would lead the way, hundreds would soon follow, most actively encouraged them. They were always treated with the utmost kindness and consideration, both by ladies and gentlemen; indeed their presence seemed to give their hosts great pleasure.

About this time, the Alexandra Native Girls School was founded, for the purpose of giving sound education to the middle classes. The rich, who were at first disinclined to spread education amongst their daughters, changed their views and decided that this was the way to go. Soon, English schools were springing up everywhere and governesses were within easy reach of all, but the adage, "All learning and no knowledge" illustrated the present state of things amongst the girls. Schooling was so successful that the girls lost interest in domestic affairs and thought their duties were summed up in attending school and gaining knowledge. This gave rise to serious complaints from those parents who were not in easy circumstances. Their daughters learned English but ignored the necessity of helping their mothers at home, while their book learning created in them an intolerable pride. They copied the extravagant dress of their rich companions, though the parents had the utmost difficulty in making ends meet. (So what else is new)?

Dosebai felt that these girls misused their education. The daughters of the rich, though they learnt the language, did not, it seemed to her, acquire the polite manners of the English. They 'walked with a peculiar thud of their boots, dangling their cambric handkerchiefs, wearing a bodice fitting tight after the English style and adorned with lace, and thus they thought themselves reformed into European ladies, but like the loud note of an empty vessel, their very appearance was enough to convince one of their limited knowledge'. Dosebai's complaints about the younger generation of educated ladies appear to sound very familiar to our present day opinions – she did not think they were proficient in household chores, cooking and needlework – well, they were taking the first steps to building a career!

From the year 1872 her little weekly parties increased, so that they mustered about twenty close friends. They visited each other frequently and met every evening at the Bandstand to converse on the topics of the day, though it was an innovation for gentlemen to stand at the carriage door and openly chat with ladies, but as on so many previous occasions this was at first ridiculed, and then imitated. In May of that year, Captain Merello of the Rubattino Steam Co. invited their whole family and friends to an entertainment on board the steamboat '*Persia*'. They, to the number of twenty, accepted this generous hospitality and spent a day of much enjoyment. Dosebai's father-in-law's sister, who had never seen, much less enjoyed an English dinner before, provoked the liveliest merriment with her comical remarks. Mistaking the decoratively dressed Italian waiters for important personages whose great courtesy led them to forget their position and serve their guests, she constantly addressed them in titles of respect and performed the most profound bowings and salaams to them.

Life continued in the same vein with holidays and balls at Government House and one fine April morning in 1875, the small company of friends set out for Mahableshwar, a beautiful hill station some 70 miles from Bombay. They halted for the night at Poona and before the break of day set off again. It was at the outset a pleasant drive in horse and carriage through hilly country, with the moon still shining, but as the day advanced it grew unbearably hot and Dosebai felt apprehensive on account of the seven young children in their party. At noon, they halted and refreshed themselves with the provisions they had brought and after resting for a couple of hours they continued on their way.

On reaching the Ghats the horses were taken out and men were yoked to their carriages, which to their eyes seemed most uncouth but apparently, these stalwart chaps found it no difficult task to pull them up the steep hillside. It took over an hour to reach the summit, where the horses were put to again, and they proceeded along a high, mountainous road full of interesting sights. They came to fields of raspberries and strawberries growing in profusion. The farmers who were emigrant Chinese, on seeing a carriage approaching, ran to them with baskets laden with these delicious fruits. As they were only obtainable in a cold or temperate zone, they had never seen them before, and their cultivation here was an index to the prevailing temperature.

Evening fell with a delicious cool breeze. The road became more and more mountainous and wild. It presented an awesome picture at dusk, with dark, jagged rocks overhanging and terrible precipices, first on one side, then on another and they were thankful when they reached journey's end at 7 pm. They established themselves in a bungalow named 'Glen Ogle', hired for the season from Mr Elias Sassoon. Their servants, who had gone before, had a good dinner ready for them and after doing it ample justice, they drowned the fatigues of this long journey in refreshing sleep.

The cold of Mahableshwar was similar to what they had heard people tell of the English spring or autumn. Early the next morning, they all set out for a walk. The paths overhung with dense foliage and the moss-covered hills clad in emerald green, made a picture so arrestingly beautiful as to throw into oblivion the dangerous impression of the previous evening. This place was truly a heavenly retreat during the hotter months, and it was to be regretted that the well-to-do natives did not avail themselves, as they should, of these healthful resorts. Some ill-founded dread prejudiced the majority from undertaking the journey. Only three or four native families had then visited this delightful haven, though it had the advantage over Matheran, both in scenery and situation, being 5000 feet above sea level. The invigorating air soon improved their walking powers, for, whereas in Bombay half a mile's walk was enough to tire one, here you could achieve three or four miles with ease.

Two other Parsi families were there at the same time, and the ladies of all three houses used to meet and form quite a procession on the early morning promenade. They made many new acquaintances among the Europeans, who were much surprised to see Goolbai riding in full English habit and the boys and girls playing Badminton together. The evenings were spent in wandering amid the stunning scenery, resting on inviting rocks where fruit and sweetmeats were enjoyed, and finishing up with a long carriage drive and dinner al fresco. On Goolbai's return from England, she frequently appeared at the Bandstand and other places of public resort in Bombay on horseback, kitted out in English riding dress. This unprecedented behaviour kindled the ire of some of the other Parsis, some of whom were so silly as to send verbal messages to her father-in-law complaining of the liberties he allowed her to take in the face of day. These wiseacres would probably have raised no objection if she had preferred to take her ride at midnight! To a Parsi, the idea of a female riding in an English habit was dissonant, although history tells us that women in Persia, where the Parsis came from, rode horses with proficiency. Their descendants, however, discarded it with fury and contempt. But with Dosebai it was otherwise – it gladdened her eyes to see her daughter enjoying this graceful exercise and her father-in-law, far from prohibiting, gave her full scope to indulge her taste for this and other healthy recreations.

Cowasji's birthday fell on one of these days, and as the Portuguese cook wasn't up to scratch with Parsi food, Dosebai took his place and prepared a most recherché repast. The special guests at dinner began to extol the Portuguese cook's skills as far beyond that of a Parsi cook; but Mr Dossabhoy remarked that the delicious dishes must have been made by some queen, so it was revealed that she was a dab hand at cookery. The gentlemen were astonished to learn that one given to such refined pursuits could also, in an emergency, fill the place of any one of her servants. Thus on this happy day, she sent a selection of her confectionery to her friends in Mahableshwar and Sir Jamsetjee complimented her by saying that it pleased him to find one so excelled in the refinements of society, possessed of the sterling qualities of a capable housewife.

These sterling qualifications were soon to be put to the test, for five or six Portuguese servants abruptly walked out, because of Mr. Pherozeshah having to severely rebuke one of them. Though there were numerous applicants for the cook's place, it was quite impossible to find one sufficiently experienced, so Dosebai had to turn her knowledge to account. Restaurants were relatively unheard of in those days and would have been little frequented by Parsis, anyway.

On 10th June, amid cooling showers of rain, they returned to Bombay on hearing of the serious illness of her father-in-law. Dosebai found domestic anarchy reigning in her own house, and was immediately engaged in setting things right there, besides which she had to pay a daily visit to her father-in-law, whose prolonged illness demanded her husband's constant attention. On the 17th July 1875 he bid adieu to this life, leaving only one son to lament him. Up to the last, he was in the full possession of his faculties. His love for her husband continued till the last.

CHAPTER 9

VISIT OF HIS ROYAL HIGHNESS THE PRINCE OF WALES 1875

It was at this time that the welcome news of the Prince of Wales' intended visit reached India, that the heir to the Crown of England was coming with royal pomp and pageantry - that was news indeed. Everyone was overjoyed at the prospect, all ages and classes were filled with joyous expectation and all equally eager to receive the respected guest with befitting honour. Indeed, it would be impossible to exaggerate the enthusiasm of the populace of Bombay. When the Duke of Edinburgh had come to India, Dosebai had felt the desire that all Her Majesty's sons might follow their brother's example, and now her wish was to be partly realised. The Native Chiefs crowded to Bombay to be presented to the fortunate English Prince and were to be seen going about the streets with their retinues of gaily clad followers. Bungalows were let at fabulous rents, all the houses were newly painted and whitewashed, streets and public gardens repaired and put in order and in every way, trade became brisk and flourishing. The city, hung with innumerable flags and bright Chinese lanterns in the trees, presented a very cheerful appearance as the day of His Royal Highness' arrival, on the *HMS Serapis* approached.

Dosebai, the biggest fan of the Royal family, put on her handsomest dress and ornaments and took her seat on one of the stands erected on the Esplanade, from where she had a good view of the Prince as he passed along, amid the deafening cheers of his exultant subjects, followed by an imposing cavalcade of Rajahs, nobles, leading citizens and high Government officials. This English Prince, coming amongst them, was considered an auspicious omen by the natives, and his presence afforded the Parsi ladies an amount of happiness and freedom unknown before; several sensible reforms arose then, amongst the native women and have been preserved ever since. For instance, widows who had hitherto been excluded from all public events, came out and participated in the general rejoicing. Others, who till this time had only driven in closed carriages with the venetian blinds tightly shut, now appeared in open carriages; some, who had never set foot in the streets were now hurrying along, eager to catch a glimpse of His Royal Highness. On the Prince's birthday, which he spent in Bombay, the illuminations were magnificent. Many a native female, throwing aside ceremony, was to be seen walking about and enjoying the sight up to a late hour. Thus it will be seen that, although the greater emancipation for native women had been advancing with slow steps since 1860, His Royal Highness' visit gave a great impetus to the movement.

On the 10th November His Royal Highness was present at a treat given to the native schoolboys and girls, where some hundreds of Parsi ladies assembled to meet him, and it was a novel feature of the entertainment that some of the most antiquated and orthodox co-religionists were to be seen there, mixing freely with the company. Dosebai saw the Prince for the last time at a Grand Review, when new colours were presented to one of the regiments. This was a very imposing spectacle, as all the Rajahs were present, their position being marked off by many coloured flags. The whole force marched past them and saluted the Prince of Wales. Through the kindness of Sir Frank Souter, she had a card of admission to the enclosure, where there were only three carriages of Parsi ladies. The Prince, attired in martial dress and seated on a beautiful steed, attracted all eyes towards him. This Grand Review was highly relished by all spectators as a representation of Royal pomp, of which until now they had only read about. Their bungalow was temporarily occupied by H.H. the Maharaja of Udaipur, where, on the occasion of the Prince of Wales paying him a visit, they had again the pleasure of seeing him.

The only thing Dosebai missed seeing was the '*HMS Serapis*', which was described to her as a vessel of extraordinary luxury. The *HMS Serapis* was a troopship, and one of five iron-hulled vessels of the Euphrates class. It must have been a beauty, 360 feet in length by about 49 feet breadth, It had a single screw, a speed of 14 knots, one funnel, a barque-rig sail plan, three 4-pounder guns and a white-painted hull. Her bow was a "ram bow" which projected forward below the waterline. She spent all of her career on the United Kingdom to India route carrying troops, a trip that averaged 70 days.

After a sojourn of a few months in various parts of India, the Prince bade adieu to the shores of India, carrying with him the heartfelt blessings of Her Majesty's loyal subjects. Again, thousands assembled at Bombay to see him and to bless him and his gracious mother.

In April 1876, Lord Lytton was appointed Governor-General and shortly after, it became generally known that Queen Victoria was about to assume the grand title of Empress of India. The entire Indian population received this news with acclamation. (This was, of course, Dosebai's account – there were quite a few with a very different opinion). An official announcement was issued, stating that the public declaration of this event would take place at a grand Durbar to be held in Delhi, the ancient capital of the Mughal Empire. Immediately, the feudatory princes, Rajahs and nobles began making arrangements to be present, and in due course set out on their way to the northern city with their large retinues and numerous followers. Preparations on a grand scale went on throughout the land and the well to do of every caste and creed were eager to be present on the occasion, as indeed they were encouraged to show their loyalty by appearing at the Durbar. It was said that something like half the population of India would be drawn towards Delhi, and that the demand for edibles of all sorts would be likely to produce a shortage. To attract the attention of the public, and to leave nothing undone that could contribute to the splendour of the ceremony, the subject was brought prominently forward everyday in all the leading native and English newspapers.

As Dosebai had long wished to travel through the various parts of India, she determined to avail herself of this favourable opportunity for visiting the historical cities of the North. Two months before the time appointed for the Durbar, she introduced the subject to her social coterie and requested her daughter and her husband to accompany her, but they did not enter into the project, being apprehensive of the greater difficulties of the journey, as well as the expenses at Delhi and en route. In the face of these discouragements, her lovely husband readily consented to the plan, saying, 'we could dispense with other company and go by ourselves.'

Accordingly, she set all necessary preparations in train and kept their intentions scrupulously secret, to ward off the storm of ridicule and scandal, which the rumour of this new departure from old custom would have triggered. She fancied she could already hear the jeering queries. 'Is it a Parsi female's business to mix in such demonstrations? How can she be so unwomanly as to venture on such a journey?' Parsi men were notoriously selfish and had monopolised for themselves every pleasure and indulgence, fancying that women were only created for household drudgery. She kept an ear to the ground to discover whether any of the noteworthy Parsi gentlemen who were honoured by an invitation to the Durbar, would take their families with them but none, apparently, dreamt of such a thing, and thus she was the more determined to go.

Watching her busily making arrangements for leaving home, her daughter and friends were given to understand that she was preparing for a sojourn at Nowsaree, a place about 150 miles distant from Bombay. Thus, everyone being on the wrong scent, she often proposed in jest that ten or twenty of their club should go to the Delhi assemblage, to which they replied, ' It is not for us to encounter such difficulties, because even if we could go to Delhi, we females would not be able to openly enjoy any of the sights'. This attitude made her laugh, but responding in the same strain, she would say 'Ah yes, a trip to Nowsaree or Gandevi is all that we women can hope for, while our husbands roll in luxury and deny themselves nothing, so, in spite of our being reputed of higher culture than many of our sisters, we lead the same dull and boring life'.

In due course, all was ready and their party of seven, comprising her husband, his old aunt of the comic disposition, their two sons, her brother Heerjeebhoy and an old trusted servant of the house, took their departure from Bombay on the 22nd December. As her husband's business affairs did not allow of a very long absence, it was necessary to have her brother's company during their tour after the Durbar was over. Prior to departure, feeling sore at the thought of enjoying so much without her daughter sharing it, she asked her again to come along but she refused, on account of the difficulties and troubles into which she thought her mother rushed willingly.

Cowasji took the management of everything most efficiently. He wrote to his cousins in Delhi to secure suitable accommodation and make all suitable arrangements for the reception of an European friend and his family whom he would accompany to Delhi. He also wrote to two friends, who were in the service of the Nizam of Hyderabad's late uncle, Amir-e-Kabir, co-regent of Hyderabad and held in high estimation. These two gentlemen were close friends and were given to understand that an European and his wife were coming. Thus, the secret was kept to the last.

Before setting out on this grand expedition, Dosebai paid a visit to her friend, Lady Sassoon, who, upon hearing of the planned journey, could not at first give credence to Dosebai's words, but on being assured that it really was so, was most delighted, saying she also would have gone if she could have found suitable lodgings there. Here, Dosebai met Lord Kilman, brother of Mrs. O.T. Burne, wife of the Private Secretary to the Viceroy of India, who also expressed himself pleased with her going to Delhi, but he did not know that she was the only Parsi lady who would be there.

On the 22nd Dec they started from *Boree Bunder* station. At 5.30 pm the train steamed out and the next day their departure for Delhi became generally known, with an announcement of the fact in the local papers. This brought many congratulatory letters from her well-meaning friends, but it cannot be denied that many others were thoroughly jealous. However, she would not allow their envy and comments to deprive her of one iota of the enjoyment placed within her reach. They reached Jubblepore the next evening at 9 pm and on alighting, her husband received a telegram, calling him back to Bombay on urgent business. This was extremely annoying, but he

65

comforted her somewhat by promising to hasten after them if his affairs allowed. He therefore parted from them, taking his youngest son, who wished to go back to Bombay with his father. They continued their journey and early the next morning, reached Allahabad. This railway station was then considered the largest and finest in India. They breakfasted there and spent the day in the city.

Hiring a carriage, they drove to the fortress, which presented a grand and imposing appearance. There was a British regiment encamped in it and much activity about the place. At a particular spot near the fortress there was a spacious subterranean cellar, which they also visited. The Hindus performed sacred rites and ceremonies here. There were human skeletons hanging up here and there and it looked dark and gruesome. They would not venture far, though other members of the group went ahead with lighted tapers and saw the vast extent of the place. To cheer themselves up, they then went to the Bazaar and discovered the much sought-after Allahabad pear. It had a sweet, delicious taste and was four times the size of those they found in Bombay, having a small stone like those of a date or greengage in the middle. They visited the confluence of the Ganges and Jumna rivers, where many Hindu devotees were bathing in the holy waters with their clothes on, and performing various religious ceremonies. The dust, however, was the prevailing element and really bothered them. At dusk, they returned to the station and enjoyed a meal prepared by their own servant. The train set off again at 9 pm, reaching Toondla the next morning. At every station, the stationmasters rendered them every possible assistance and attention. They unanimously declared that thousands of passengers had passed through their station on the way to Delhi, but that they had never seen a Parsi lady till she came along. The English passengers freely commented upon her appearance, till they became aware that she could talk their language, thus many new friendships sprang up in the course of this journey.

At this station two new passengers entered their carriage, one of whom was a barrister practising at Cawnpore and the other was the Principal of the Martiniere College at Lucknow. The amusing conversation that they carried on together caused Dosebai to smile, whereupon the man of learning whispered to his friend of the long robe that he thought she understood what they were saying. The other retorted that such a grown-up Parsi lady was certainly not so accomplished. This created much merriment and they were soon chatting together like old friends. The nearer they got to Delhi, the more the number of passengers increased, so that the crowding and bustle of the last hour were such as to throw into oblivion the troubles of the preceding three days journey; however, by God's grace, they arrived safely at their destination.

Delhi Durbar

CHAPTER 10

THE DELHI DURBAR AND THE PROCLAMATION 1877

At Delhi station the great concourse of people, the shouting and excitement made her think that the timorous folk of Bombay were not so far wrong, that this was really no place for a native female to be in, especially without her husband. But she soon caught sight of her husband's cousin, Mr Edulji Cowasji Jamsetji hurrying towards them, and her courage revived. This 'friend in need' had made all the fitting arrangements for the reception of an English lady and gentleman, whom her husband was to accompany and had come to the station to await them. He was glad that his exertions had been made on Dosebai's behalf and steering them skilfully through the great crowd, he drove them to a small bungalow in the compound of the United Service Hotel, which he had secured for the supposedly English couple. Though the miniature bungalow was cabin-like in its dimensions, it was nicely furnished and answered all their requirements, but the cold was so severe that she was glad to bring into requisition the extra bedding they had brought with them.

Early the next morning, she was awoken by someone knocking on her door. This turned out to be a Hindu clerk in the service of H.H. The Amir-i-Kabir, co-regent of Hyderabad; the poor man had been on their trail all night and was glad to have found them at last. The explanation of the matter was that, on her husband's return from Jubblepore, he had telegraphed her arrival to his kind and good friend Mr. Shapoorjee, but the message arriving too late, he had failed to meet her at the station and had employed this clerk to find out their whereabouts. Shortly afterwards, his brother, Mr. Jamsetjee, arrived in his carriage. He insisted on their leaving the Hotel and making use of the beautiful tents they had erected for them in the complex of the Delhi Durbar. She thanked him kindly but resolved to stay where they were.

On the 26th they had a long drive in Mr. Shapoorjee's open mail phaeton drawn by a pair of beautiful studs, through the principal thoroughfares of the city and wherever they looked, dense crowds of people were to be seen, to whom the sight of a Parsi lady was a novelty. Thus, they reached the immense *Maidan* (open space), studded with innumerable tents, in preparation for the Delhi Durbar. Here, they saw two of those tents that Mr. Shapoorjee had so kindly provided for their use. They were most comfortable and inviting, supplied with every convenience and although Dosebai was most appreciative, she excused herself from accepting the accommodation on account of the extreme cold that would have been experienced in such an open and unprotected plain. They re-entered the city through the lofty and spacious Kashmir and Lucknow gates, once no doubt grand and imposing, but now falling into decay. Proceeding through streets teeming with people, they came to Chandni-Chowk, flanked on each side by houses. There were a great many Hindus and Mahomedans, and a few Parsis, who were taken by surprise on seeing her drive through this city of antiquity in an open carriage, and the gaping crowd that gathered round the carriage made it a matter of difficulty to proceed. She heard several passing their opinion as to her identity. Some said she was an European, some took her for a Chinese, some for an Egyptian, a Turkish lady and so on, but very few knew her as a Parsi, as they could not believe that a Parsi lady would venture through such populous thoroughfares in an open carriage.

It was exceedingly droll to listen to the rejoinders made by her old aunt to these openly expressed opinions. She did not hesitate to scold the curious crowd saying, 'If you want to see persons like us, come to Bombay'. The general astonishment with which they were beheld wherever they went in this city, was due to the gaily coloured saris they wore and to the fact that none of the native women had ever been in an open carriage as according to custom, they never appeared in public nor went from one place to another without being caged up in a carriage with all blinds closed.

That evening, Mr. Shapoorjee came to take them sightseeing again. They saw several princes and Rajahs with their retinues, and also some of the handsome four-in-hand coaches of Englishmen. Of these, the turnout of the Lieutenant Governor attracted most attention from its novelty. The State carriage was drawn by six camels ridden by grooms in gorgeous livery much bedecked with gold fringe and silver lace; in the carriage, which was a large open brake, a number of beautiful young ladies were seated. This unique show was very striking to them, but apparently more so to her old aunty who, in the exuberance of her delight, showered blessings on Dosebai for having afforded her such enjoyments at her advanced age.

On the way back, they saw several ancient buildings, the most remarkable being the Delhi fortress of gigantic magnitude. The strength and stability of this ancient fortification, some of which had been destroyed by war, proved that the architects of old understood the secret of setting time and decay at defiance. They had a grand view of the Juma Masjid, the largest mosque in India. The clouds of dust somewhat marred their enjoyment, although the roads were being constantly watered so as to present a fresh, monsoon appearance. A cold breeze and thick fog came on and the accompanying darkness rendered it necessary for them to return home by 7 o'clock. Mr. Shapoorjee and his brother made their way as best as they could, back to their tents, carrying with them grateful thanks for the delightful and interesting drive.

On the morning of the 27th they started for an early walk but had to beat a hasty retreat. The cold was more than they could bear. After dressing themselves in layers of warm woollen garments and enveloping themselves in long overcoats such as European ladies wore, they ventured forth again and took a brisk walk, which soon made them warm and comfortable.

They arranged with the Hotel Manager to have a carriage and pair retained for their use besides which, Mr.Shapoorjee placed another carriage and horses at their disposal. On Thursday the 28th they headed out early in the morning, towards the gardens of the city, where the tombs and monuments of rich nobles who flourished in the past were daily strewn with fresh flowers and fragrant herbs. Later that morning Dosebai started, in company with her brother, to pay a visit to the Honourable Mrs. Burne in the Viceroy's camp. Unfortunately, they forgot to carry the guidebook for this vast encampment and therefore had much trouble and unnecessary fatigue before they could find her tent. She was most kindly received by Mrs. Burne, who invited her to a supper party and also asked her to come and be presented to Lady Lytton in the evening.

Returning home, Dosebai selected suitable garments for the visit to Her Excellency and at half past four, drove with her son to the Viceroy's tents in a splendid carriage and pair lent for the occasion by the aforementioned Mr. Hormusjee, but in consequence of the circuitous route which had to be taken, the appointed hour was long past when they reached their goal and Lady Lytton and Mrs. Burne had gone out. So they had to return in disappointment. On the way, they saw several Rajahs with their retinues and had an opportunity of learning something of the intricacies of the vast encampment. The streets were more crowded than ever, indeed every day seemed to increase the number of the populace.

Later that evening, while sitting reading the newspaper of the day in which was detailed everything going on in Delhi, a trooper rode up with a note from the Viceroy's camp. It was from kind Mrs. Burne, regretting having missed Dosebai's visit and hoping she would arrange another time for being presented to Lady Lytton.

The following morning Dosebai wished to go out for her usual walk and those of her party who could not, on account of the cold, easily shake off sleep, were cajoled into doing so by the diligent use of a pin for she was anxious not to lose a single hour when there was so much of interest to be seen. (How did her friends put up with this lady)? First walking to Mr. Shapoorjee's, where they had a cup of tea, they drove to the vast plain where the native princes and chiefs were encamped and they could not help but admire the orderly distribution of these quarters.

Even the horses, elephants and camels were comfortably established in separate tents and signboards were set up here and there with the name of the Rajah, whose tents adjoined. Many of

71

these tents, particularly those of the Viceroy and his staff, and of H.H. the Nizam, were more like palaces; immensely spacious, well built, well furnished and well lit. Others were fitted up as places of leisure, others again as places of business, telegraph office and so on, and yet nothing gave the impression of newness or temporariness, for every tent was covered with evergreen creepers and surrounded by tastefully laid out gardens. Wells were sunk here and there, and all the paths were sprinkled with sand. At every turning, rows of artillery met you and colourful flags bearing distinctive designs floated over high officials' quarters.

The tents were fitted with fireplaces and chimneys and the fire had to be kept continually burning, as the weather was so cold. They were all tastefully decorated and in the evening, when lit up, they presented a very brilliant appearance. It would need the descriptive powers of a novelist coupled with the imaginative mind of a poet to do justice to the scene. They could not but feel intense admiration for the organising genius of the English, who, in the short space of three months, had converted a barren plain into this highly organised city of tents, set down in a smiling garden.

Though India boasted of many noble chiefs, Dosebai doubted if one could be found who would bring order out of chaos as the English did, at all events a native ruler would take years to do it. Good substantial roads were constructed all the way up the hill, from which point one had a good view of the labyrinthine encampment. To assist the public, a directory had been published giving the street, number and name of the occupant of each tent, but even then it was no easy task to find one's way. In the afternoon of this day they went to the Exhibition, which, considering the former condition of the city, was quite creditable. The entire collection represented local talent, most noticeable being the exquisite miniature paintings on ivory, copper and brassware and of course, jewellery.

As they headed back at 5 o'clock, the crowd was absolutely massive. They met on their drive, the imposing cavalcade of H.H. the Nizam of Hyderabad, headed by his illustrious and accomplished premier Sir Salar Jung; then came the tightly closed carriages of the

Begums or royal ladies, followed by a train of elephants, with gold and silver howdahs on their backs in which were accommodated a number of beautifully dressed European ladies. Then came a file of camels. Several Rajahs were to be seen driving in their ornate carriages, preceded and followed by a number of retainers on horses. In the two-horse State carriage it was difficult to distinguish, from amongst the four or six men all sitting with their legs tucked under them, which one was the Rajah but the profusion of jewellery worn by one of the number generally solved the problem.

It was impossible to witness all the splendour and display of wealth then reigning in Delhi without feeling how powerful was the sceptre of Queen Victoria, Empress of the land. Next morning on their early walk, they met several parties of Europeans. A few Rajahs and Nawabs were to be seen either on horseback or borne along at a slow pace on the backs of elephants. She had heard of the arrival of some of the Parsi aristocracy, but saw none on account, no doubt, of the inclement weather. She was in a dilemma, as her brother, Heerjeebhoy, could not get a card of admission to the Durbar though, through Mrs. Burne's kindness she had secured several places for herself in special reserved seats and in consequence had written to her husband and eldest brother to come, and go with her to the assemblage. To her chagrin, her husband could not get away, but her brother telegraphed that he was coming. On offering Heerjeebhoy one of her cards, he declined to take it, as her name, not his, was on it and he testily expressed that he could readily obtain one for himself from Major Borass with whom he was on an intimate footing.

Mr. Eduljee had kindly obtained permission for them to see the fortress and on their way there, they visited Juma Masjid, with its massive gateway and marble court stairs, sculptures and baths. They were lost in wonder at this grand work of antiquity, its vast hall capable of accommodating between three and four thousand people. The minarets of white marble and the whole edifice presented an ideal of beauty and sublimity. A beautiful marble wall encircled the extensive compound, with graceful arches at intervals.

73

They returned at 4 o'clock to allow for her brother's visit to Major Borass to ask for a card of admission which, however, in spite of his arguments and sophistry he failed to obtain, and so returned very much out of humour, so much so that he proposed that Dosebai should not appear at the Durbar. Seeing him so unreasonable, she kept silent and presently proceeded to the tent of her worthy friend Mrs. Burne. She was, unfortunately, not at home, so Dosebai left a message to the effect that, as her husband was not with her, she should be glad of her brother's company at the Grand Durbar, as it would be impossible for her to go alone. Leaving her brother's name on her card, she returned to the hotel.

Later that day, she set out, with her aunt, to see the staging where the Durbar was to be held. Although this building was only to be of momentary use, thousands had been spent on its erection and decoration. The pillars were of gold and silver, expensive and exquisite carpets were spread on the floor and a costly canopy of velvet, with a golden fringe, was hung up above. The front seats consisted of rich sofas and chairs, upholstered in blue satin and white silk cord and tassels. Only twenty-five persons could be accommodated on the dais, which was elaborately carved and richly ornamented. The whole scene was like a magic panorama conjured up by genii. Her elderly aunt was fairly bewildered by the magnificence and exclaimed, 'Methinks, it is a specimen of Paradise which I see before me'. (Well, words to that effect).

Driving out in the evening, they saw a great concourse of people in the main thoroughfares, flags hung from every nook and corner and there was a splendid display of regimental uniforms. Lord Lytton, whose lustrous equipage altogether eclipsed those of the Indian princes, appeared presently in view, when every European uncovered his head, handkerchiefs were waved and the Rajahs salaamed with both hands. To these salutations of respect, Lord Lytton responded with a graceful inclination of the head. On Dosebai's return, she found a kind note from Mrs. Burne, saying she had sent up her name, along with her brother's, to the Military Secretary and she hoped they would soon receive another ticket.

On the 1st January 1877, rising ridiculously early, that is to say – five in the morning, they found much life and activity at the hotel and the day's proceedings were the subject of excitement. Her brother Dorabjee was amongst the arrivals and both he and her son were to accompany her to the assemblage. After breakfast at nine, they drove off in two carriages, her aunt and some members of the party stopping at Mr. Shapoorjee's tent, whence they could command a view of the procession and the others continuing on their way to the Durbar tent, but so huge was the crowd of people and vehicles, that although the road was broad enough for six carriages to drive abreast, wheels and horses were brought into close proximity with each other and they could only proceed at a snail's pace.

The road was lined with alternate companies of infantry and cavalry and the police were indefatigable in preserving order and keeping the way clear. Around the complex there was a circle of several magnificent elephants, gaily caparisoned with uniform howdahs on their backs, drawn up to look like a castle wall and seated in the howdahs, were the handsomely clad followers of the Indian Princes. Further on, there was a detachment of English cavalry, whose handsome appearance and gorgeous equipment were much admired. Standing shoulder to shoulder in statue-like rigidity, so as to form a safe passage for the Princes, was a detachment of English infantry and well spaced out there were military bands, the sound of brass adding to the excitement of the occasion.

Passing slowly along, they reached the steps of the amphitheatre at noon, but it was with difficulty that they made their way through the dense crowd on the stairs. On entering the tent, an officer came up and taking their cards, conducted them to their seats. Dosebai was apportioned a very conspicuous place in the front row amongst leading officials and their ladies. To her left sat the Portuguese Governor-General of Goa and on the right, Lady Staveley, wife of the Commander-in-Chief of Bombay. Dosebai's brother sat immediately behind her. A portion of the interior was reserved for the Zenana (Muslim) ladies who were screened from view by heavy curtains and had taken their seats at an early hour of the morning before curious eyes were open. A little further along were the Indian

Princes, the first and foremost among whom was H.H. the infant Nizam of Hyderabad with his able minister Salar Jung, and his uncle the co-regent Amir-i-Kabir. There were also the Maharajahs Gaekwar, Scindia, and Holkar, the rulers of Mysore and Kashmir, the Begum of Bhopal and others, all seated according to their rank and precedence with their banners waving above them.

Such a princely gathering had never been known in the annals of India. All these Rajahs wore rare ornaments, diamonds as large as a sovereign hung from their ears and their breasts were ablaze with rubies and emeralds in necklaces which literally covered them; their hands and arms glittered with rings and diamond-studded bracelets, their turbans were mounted in gold and bedecked with pearls and diamonds and their rapiers and sword hilts were beautifully engraved and set with precious stones. When a ray of the midday sun happened to light on any of these gorgeous personages it dazzled one's eyes to look at them. Their dresses were correspondingly splendid and the sum represented upon their persons must have amounted to millions.

At half past twelve, Lord Lytton made his stately appearance and took his seat on the dais. He met with an enthusiastic reception, the entire assemblage rising to do him homage. At that moment the scene was most brilliant and striking, the band played, the soldiers presented arms and the diamonds shone with oscillating splendour amid the rich hues of the ladies' and Rajahs' raiment. Precisely at one o'clock, Colonel Thornton came forward and read in a clear sonorous tone the Royal Proclamation, wherein the humane policy of the Government was set forth and Her Majesty's Resolution from that day forth to assume the title and dignity of Empress of India or Kaiser-i-Hind. Then the National Anthem pealed forth, followed by the royal salute of one hundred and one guns and a *feu-de-joie* from the infantry. With the clouds of smoke the atmosphere became murky, the elephants and the horses took fright and several accidents occurred. Serious mischief was however, averted as it had been expected, the crowd being absolutely enormous.

At about 2 pm the people began to disperse, but what with the interminable cavalcade of the Rajahs and the dense mass of humanity impeding the way, it was 5 o'clock before they entered their carriage and half past six before they reached home. This was an unbelievably spectacular and hugely memorable experience, indeed.

The following morning, Mrs Burne and her brother Lord Kilman called on Dosebai. Mrs. Burne invited her to lunch and asked when she would like to come and meet Lady Lytton. She also offered Dosebai tickets to see the fireworks, which were to take place that night but in reply to all her kind enquiries, Dosebai informed her that she was truly unwell, probably a result of the huge amount of dust everywhere and the extreme cold. After the departure of her kind visitors, she had a serious relapse, which meant that she needed to quit Delhi without delay. She would be able to procure some special medicine in Agra. Accordingly, she made up her mind to go to Agra, so that in the event of regaining her health, she could see the celebrated Taj Mahal.

That evening at dinner with a glass of champagne, they pledged Her Majesty's health as well as that of the hundreds of Indian Princes who had congregated there. Then, wrapping themselves up warmly, they left their comfortable little cabin and drove to the station. The streets and houses were splendidly illuminated in honour of the Proclamation and their last look at the grand old city was a favourable one. The number of travellers at the station was so immense that half had to turn back, but by the assistance of their worthy cousin, Mr. Eduljee, they were soon installed in a carriage and ready for the start. Tired but happy, they steamed out of the Imperial city, viewing from the train the gleaming white marble Juma Masjid in the light of innumerable bonfires.

CHAPTER 11

THE TAJ MAHAL
AND
A VISIT TO LUCKNOW

The train was crowded to excess but seated in their first class carriage, they felt no discomfort and their fellow passengers were very polite. Arriving at Agra early in the morning, they found the cold less severe than at Delhi. They hired a vehicle called a '*Yekko*', to which one horse with a crested cap over its head, was yoked and drove to their lodgings, a sumptuous residence reserved for the use of the co-regent of Hyderabad, Amir-i-Kabir. However, as he was not expected for some time, Mr. Shapoorjee had got permission for its temporary occupation. Soon after lunch, they set off to see the wonderful Taj Mahal.

The first impression of this world-renowned edifice was one of utter amazement. On entering the arched gateway, the pure white marble, dazzling in the light of the midday sun, burst upon their gaze in all its lustrous majesty. It certainly was a noble structure and well illustrated the lavish and fantastic taste of the old Moghul Empire. The approach was paved with huge blocks of marble, uniform in size and colour. Here and there, large cisterns of water stood beneath an umbrageous canopy of green, lending an air of calm and coolness to the scene. Proceeding up a noble flight of marble stairs, they entered a spacious court surrounded by a low wall. The Taj Mahal itself stood in the centre of this enclosure or *chowk*, and at its four corners stately minarets reared themselves aloft, their height exceeding that of the Cathedral tower of Bombay or even the Colaba Lighthouse. Entering the Mausoleum, a series of highly polished marble steps led to a platform just under the dome, and below this there was a staircase to the vault, which was the last resting place of Mumtaz Mahal (whose real birth name was Arjumand Banu), the beloved queen of Shah Jehan, who built this magnificent monument devoted to her memory.

The intricate relief carving on the white marble of the interior was marvellous and realistically represented flowers, trees, and birds, pillars of coloured marble sustained the roof and the floor was studded with small pieces of bright marble to represent precious stones. Provided with lit tapers, they descended to the vault and beheld the last resting place of the once beautiful queen. The sarcophagus was a rare specimen of elaborate carving. It was enveloped in a velvet coverlet embroidered in gold and silk and the whole was surmounted by a canopy of fresh flowers. Frankincense and other aromatic herbs were kept continually burning and the air was heavy with their fragrance. All who entered the vault made an offering of gold or silver coins according to their means. They much admired the spacious baths, supplied with hot and cold water and the old aunt (of seventy-five), climbed to the top of one of the lofty minarets so as to see everything there was to see.

In Dosebai's own words, 'If there be anything on earth which can to a slight extent illustrate the beauty of Paradise, surely it must be this unrivalled building. Hundreds of people must have been employed for many years and the chaste white marble, inlaid with gems, must have cost a fabulous sum. It seems as if the art and skills of these older days are extinct. Under British rule, large and showy architecture springs up as if by magic, the object being to get it finished in the shortest time possible, but nothing approaching the exquisite detail and costly elegance of the Taj Mahal has been attempted in modern times. It is now in charge of the British Government and kept so well in order that it has the appearance of being recently built.

They left Agra the next evening heading for Lucknow and the following morning, arrived at Cawnpore. After a halt of two hours at Cawnpore, the junction of the Oudh and Rohilkund Railways, they boarded the train for Lucknow. Their friend Mr. Hormusjee met them at the station, leading them to the refreshment room, where a sumptuous breakfast was waiting and after duly appreciating it they seated themselves in their host's carriage and drove to his hotel, passing through the principal streets on the way. The Prince of Wales Hotel, of which Mr. Hormusjee was sole proprietor, suited their taste and convenience exactly, and the suite of handsomely furnished rooms set apart for them left nothing to be desired and made Dosebai feel thoroughly at home.

After refreshing themselves with a hot bath they rested from the fatigues of the journey. The climate was most agreeable and when lunch was announced at 12 o'clock they approached the table with considerably improved appetites. The cuisine, a fusion of English and Mughal tastes, was excellent and better than that to which they were habituated even at home, and her aunt relished her dinner exceedingly, expressing her opinion that even the most skilled Parsi cook in Bombay could not produce such delicious dishes. At one o'clock they retired to rest; at two they had tea and biscuits and at three they drove out with Mr. Hormusjee in a carriage and pair to see the city.

The Kaiserbagh was built between 1848 and 1850 by Wajid Ali Shah, who had very grandiose ideas. It was in a large enclosure with gates of palatial dimensions at the four sides. These gates were of iron, wonderfully painted and engraved with figures of lions, tigers and fantasy creatures with outstretched wings. Entering one of these magnificent gateways, one approached the *Baradari* in the centre, a large, square, white stone structure that had originally been covered entirely in pure silver. The architecture of the whole edifice was a mixture of east and west, with ionic columns, Moghul style minarets and Hindu lanterns and umbrella shapes, and several European statues for good measure. Unusual, to say the least. Broad roads, bordered with trees and water tanks, led them to the opposite gate, where they crossed a handsome bridge over the Jumna River, from which they could command a fine view of the city and its surrounding plains. On the way back to the hotel their kind host entertained them with amusing tales of the city.

It was *Muharram* (a Muslim festival of mourning to commemorate the Battle of Karbala) when they were at Lucknow and all the mosques were highly decorated. Attached to every mosque there were bathing places, supplied with hot and cold water which were not exclusively reserved for the worshippers as any one could have a bath on payment of the tariff, and if only one bath was wanted, as many as four attendants came to await your orders. Dosebai could not but wonder, on seeing this, why Bombay was altogether without such admirable public baths. Taking into account the wealth and enterprise of the Bombay Muslims, as compared with the poverty of a large number of the race in Lucknow, the generosity of the latter was far beyond what one witnessed during the *Muharram* festival in Bombay.

Feeling very tired on their return late at night, they would have rested but for the desire to leave nothing of interest unseen and therefore started out again, very early the next morning. They drove to the Muchibagh (Park), within which the celebrated fortress of Chattar Manzil is situated. The fort was fairly ruined, dilapidated but one could see the plain and solid structure of the fortifications. The ground floor had been used as a magazine and had withstood many attacks. They climbed up to the highest point and had a bird's-eye view of Lucknow and its ancient walls. Near the Fortress there was a large, artificial pond with stone steps leading down to the water, surrounded by caravansaries for the use of the travellers who came to bathe there. They returned at half past two, much fatigued by the climbing of the fortress, but after having refreshed themselves they set off yet again. Mr. Hormusjee's splendid carriage and his English coachman were always waiting for them with fresh horses at the appointed hour, no matter how inconvenient it seemed.

They now drove to the Residency, in the large cellars of which, the wives and children of the English officers had taken refuge at the time of the Mutiny in 1857, and the appearance of the outer walls showed that it must have been heavily bombarded at one time. It saddened Dosebai to think that, in that gloomy subterranean place into which not a ray of light could penetrate even at midday, a multitude of tender ladies and children had hidden for four days.

81

There was much to accomplish, so next they set out to see the old part of Lucknow. The gates of Great Imambara, supported on high, massive pillars of stone, impressed them by their graceful, artistic character and the tomb and gate of Husseinabad were also worthy of note. From there, they proceeded to the Martiniere College and while being shown over its extensive premises, who should they meet, but their fellow passenger of the journey to Delhi. He expressed his pleasure at meeting them again and showed them the whole of the school and introduced them to his wife and children. Nor was this all, he also offered them wine and fruit and for his kindness and courtesy they were most appreciative.

This school originated in a piece of romance. It was founded by Major General Claude Martin who was born in Lyon, France. He rose from the rank of a common soldier to one of the highest military posts in India. Much of his life was spent in Lucknow, where he married a Muslim girl. He was blessed with an only son, but on the decree of an all-wise providence, his beloved wife and idolised child died before him. He died in 1800 in Lucknow and his will bequeathed the whole of his fortune to the endowment of this noble institution. Portraits of this distinguished philanthropist, his wife and son were hung up in the school and his memory would ever be held dear in India. The school afforded an excellent and advanced education and accommodated a number of boarders but the students were all away for the Christmas vacation at that time of year.

They returned to the hotel at one o'clock and as they intended to leave Lucknow the following day, they sat down to lunch for the last time. Dosebai, in a short toast, gave expression to the great pleasure she had derived from her visit to this town and offered her most sincere and warm thanks for the favours heaped upon them by their worthy host. She gave orders for their luggage to be packed and ready, and set off again at 2 o'clock to see the Museum, and several other places that had escaped them in their former rambles.

Mr. Hormusjee had made ready for this final and rather special excursion, an elephant with a howdah, in which four of them were accommodated. Her old aunty found it rather difficult to mount to this lofty perch but succeeded at last, and took her place in the howdah with considerable pride. They found an elephant ride a most amusing experience. The huge creature threaded his way through the narrow, crowded streets, nothing disturbing his equanimity or causing him to alter his pace. They could easily see into the dwellings as they passed along and they created no little stir amongst their occupants; some ran to see them, others would have liked to question them from their balconies and others, with a salute of the hands would call out to them in their patois, 'Begum' (Princess), 'pray stop awhile and do such poor people as we are, the honour of partaking of our *pan-sopari* (betel nut and leaves), for we never saw such a thing before as a Begum riding on an elephant in public'. The aunt was highly amused by the sensation they created and talked to the people in the garrulous fashion of the aged. (That was Dosebai's choice of word, by which she probably meant 'confident and friendly'). Crowds of pedestrians began to gather around the elephant in the middle of the street, but as there was a total disregard of sanitation and cleanliness in this quarter of Lucknow and as there issued from the baker's shops nauseating odours of rank oil and meats in the process of being baked, they were glad to hurry along into purer air. This singularly pleasant elephant ride was a fitting end to their visit.

Rising on the 10th and bidding farewell to the Prince of Wales Hotel, they drove off to the station and steamed out of Lucknow at nine in the morning, bound for the sacred city of the Hindus, Benares.

83

CHAPTER 12

BENARES – THE SACRED CITY OF INDIA
AND
CALCUTTA –THE CITY OF PALACES

What Jerusalem was to the Christians, Benares was to the Hindus. Its temples were famous and attracted hundreds of thousands of pilgrims every year. Settling into the Traveller's Bungalow, they rested awhile and then went out for a drive. The hired horses were lean and miserable, and their pace slower than that of a Bombay bullock. They were disappointed with the temples they passed as they proceeded further to the Bazaar. On seeing the so-called 'Golden Temple', built of stone and surmounted by a shining dome, not as one would suppose, covered with plates of gold but some inferior metal highly burnished, they were again, unimpressed. Hindu devotees from all parts of India flocked here to perform their holy rites. The lane leading to the Golden Temple was so muddy that they could not avoid soiling all their clothing. They had to make their way through a crowd of mendicants in dirty, stinking garments and what with this, and the disgusting odours filling the air, it was literally unbearable and they fled away.

Next on the list was another temple infested with monkeys. The precincts were no better, but at least they enjoyed watching the frolics of these cute animals. The city of Golden Temples did not answer to the expectations that its pompous title conjured up as it was full of filth and squalor, excepting in that portion where European regiments were encamped. They returned to the bungalow for tea and made up their minds to leave this city, where the most striking features were heaps of rubbish and pools of mud.

That evening, they left the Traveller's Bungalow and in order to reach the railway station, had to cross a floating bridge. The currents in the river were considerable and their carriage had to cross at a very slow, walking pace. Bidding adieu to Benares, they took the train for Mogul-Serai, where they halted for the night. As the first train for Calcutta started at ten o'clock the next evening, they had time to see something of the town before they left, the servant meanwhile cooking fresh dishes for the journey. After dinner at the station hotel they entered the train again, travelled all night and reached Calcutta at daybreak.

The train steamed into the majestic Howrah Station at Calcutta at 8 am. Set Manekjee Rustomjee, along with several members of his family, was there to receive them. On the way to their residence they crossed the mighty bridge over the Hooghly River. The cooling breeze from the river was very refreshing and from here, they had a view of the many notable buildings of Calcutta. They passed the handsome gateway of Government House and soon reached their friend's mansion in Chowringhee Road, where Bai Sakerbai gave them a cordial welcome. Not having met for twelve years, they were mutually pleased to see each other again. Their rooms were most inviting, looking out on the Esplanade.

After breakfast, they went up to an open balcony on the first floor, from which a panoramic view of Calcutta was to be had. There was Government House standing on the Esplanade, in front of which, the main thoroughfare of Chowringhee runs, and all the way along the stately homes of the aristocracy were discernible.

Calcutta was a magnificent city. After tea at 3 pm, they dressed for an evening drive, the carriage and pair of their host accommodating his two daughters, named Pherozebai and Dhunbai, Dosebai and her aunt. They drove towards the Oval where the Eden garden and Bandstand were located. This promenade could be driven round three or four times in an hour and was pleasantly situated on the banks of the Hooghly. In the distance, many a stately ship lay anchored. This being a fashionable evening resort, many wealthy Baboos (wealthy Bengalis), with uncovered heads and in plainest muslin dress were to be seen driving their splendid carriages. The older people adhered to their primitive national dress consisting of a '*dagog*' around their waist and a thin muslin covering thrown over their shoulders but the younger generation, calling themselves reformers, wore coat, trousers and cap after the English style. Returning at 7 pm they sat down to dinner at which the mirth that prevailed was even more relished than the choice dainties set before them by their gentle hostess.

The next morning, the 13th, Dosebai woke at seven and found her hostess preparing tea with her own hands. This was much to Dosebai's taste as all the ingredients were duly proportioned and she had not met with so good a drink anywhere throughout her journey. Unlike Indians in those days her friend made tea herself, like an European lady, and prided herself upon the excellence of her infusion; for Dosebai's part, let it be sufficient praise to say that another cup would not have been unwelcome.

Lunch was served promptly at one o'clock everyday at which the variety and prettiness of the dishes was astonishing. After this meal, Dosebai generally retired to her room to write letters to Bombay and rest awhile. Four o'clock was tea-time after which they went for a drive. When any European or native person of importance passed them on the promenade, he was pointed out to them. Thus one day she saw Sir Ashley Eden the Lieutenant Governor, of whom she had frequently heard. Many wealthy Jews and Armenians passed them in their open carriages with their ladies, elegantly attired in European costumes. The carriage in which they were seated being a brougham, they could not so well enjoy the scene as if it had been an open vehicle, but as their host's family, as well as that of the few other Parsis domiciled in Calcutta never appeared in an open carriage, Dosebai had no recourse but to conform to their ways.

On the 14th January 1877 in company with Pherozbai, Lady Sassoon and her daughter Mrs. Ezra, she paid a visit to Mr. Joseph. His establishment she found equally magnificent as that of his father in Bombay and he had, moreover, adopted all the English manners and customs. The same day they visited the Court House Museum and other buildings of importance, all of which they found most interesting and far superior to those of Bombay. Returning via the

European quarter, they were cheered by the strains of the band and the sight of Lord and Lady Lytton driving in state, receiving the salutations of the subjects of Her Majesty the Queen Empress.

Next morning, Dosebai was told that the sons of the house had gone to escort Set Byramjee of Bombay from the railway station. In due course, he arrived with a number of his friends. Thus the number of guests increased everyday under this hospitable roof and the conversation at the dinner table was highly animated. Though this was a rainy day that was spent indoors, the time sped on quickly and pleasantly.

On the 17th afternoon, Mrs. Ezra and her friend called upon them. Mrs Ezra showed Dosebai much kindness in many ways, besides most considerately placing her carriage and horses at her disposal. In the evening they drove to several beautifully kept public gardens and also to the Zoological gardens, where they had the supreme satisfaction of seeing the statues of eminent statesmen and generals of whom they had frequently read in books, and who, by a judicious use of their authority, had spread peace and prosperity over the land in times gone by. (So why were they displayed in the Zoological Gardens)?

On the 18th Mrs. Ezra came to take Dosebai to the mansion of her husband's parents, which was situated in the commercial part of the town, where old Mr Ezra lived with his family. This locality reminded Dosebai of Bombay thirty years ago. At that time there was a street in the Fort known as Mapla Street, inhabited solely by the Jews, whither she used to accompany her mother, when she went to visit Mr. Moses, the brother-in-law of Sir Albert Sassoon, and his wife. Mrs Ezra's mother-in-law was of good social bearing and wore the ancient dress peculiar to her race, though her daughters and daughters-in-law were in English costume. They offered them a light repast of dried Persian fruits, fresh ripe fruits of Calcutta, homemade sweetmeats, coffee and syrups, which of course, they thoroughly enjoyed. They entered into lively conversation, in the course of which Dosebai expressed her satisfaction at seeing so many modern reforms adopted by the children of the chosen race.

She could not help contrasting the prevalence of old customs in this millionaire's house with the thoroughly avant-garde European taste prevalent at the residence of her son. It may be to the credit of old Mr. Ezra that he not only allowed but actively encouraged his children to adopt whatever reasonable innovation they may affect, as befits a most affectionate father. Young Mrs. Ezra had had the benefit of a sound English education in her parents' house and being of an urbane disposition, she shone wherever she appeared and lived in the most complete harmony with the different members of her husband's family.

Later that afternoon they accompanied Bai Sakerbai on visits to several of the rich and worthy citizens of Calcutta. One residence, known as 'Seven Lakes' was specially worthy of mention for, within its spacious grounds, there were seven enormous reservoirs filled with flowing water and provided with boats. In the midst of the garden, with dense green foliage fringing the lakes, stood the prettiest bungalow. It was sumptuously furnished and Dosebai would have stayed here forever, enjoying this delightful retreat, where Nature and Art had combined in perfection.

On the 19th she went to Government House to see her friend Mrs. Burne, but she was not at home. In the course of the evening, Dosebai was much grieved to hear that she was in deep mourning on account of the death of her beloved sister. This afternoon, all Set Manekjee's guests were invited to the highly ornamental residence of one of his wealthy Baboo friends. They found the Baboo at home, and great as his riches might have been, they found his simplicity even greater. He was very unassuming in his attire, for he wore only a thin, richly worked muslin covering. He was the happy father of seven sons, who like him, were civil and good-natured and well versed in different arts. Unlike the greater number of Parsis of the day, these seven young Bengalees were neither spoilt by their wealth nor undutiful to their father. On the contrary, each delighted to do him honour, and in the palatial residence which was still in course of construction each gave the best he had to offer to their father – one son was an artist, another an architect, the third a botanist and the rest attended to the affairs of their father.

This noble citizen was none other than Rai Rajendranath Malek. His magnificent home had already been ten years in course of erection and it was said that a similar period would elapse before it could be completed. It was built of pure polished marble of the same ivory white as that of the Taj Mahal. The threshold of each room was made to represent flowers, leaves and birds, while the floor of the room shone in varied coloured marble. The ceiling was decorated with parrots and other birds in bright colours and gold leaf. The pillars in this magnificent edifice were of black, tawny and white marble. There were many statues of deities and several oil paintings of His Imperial Majesty's family done by the artist son and alabaster statues of Indian Princes and Princesses. At the rear of the castle there was a curiously carved temple bearing pious inscriptions in gold and silver and adorned with fragrant flowers. In the beautifully laid out gardens there was a rare collection of birds, such as parrots, cockatoos, peacocks and many others of graceful plumage and also, a number of animals the like of which they had never seen anywhere else. They spent much time in wandering around this wildly ostentatious palace and took leave of its master thanking him heartily for his courtesy and trouble.

On coming down to breakfast the next morning, they heard the news that Set Dinshawjee Manekjee Petit of Bombay was arriving with a host of friends, and would also be staying in their friend's mansion. Several Parsi Sethias who had been present at the Delhi assemblage extended their tour as Dosebai had done, in order to see Calcutta, but the idea of sharing their enjoyment with their fair partners never for one moment entered their heads. Thus it will be understood that the bold step which Dosebai had taken created some ill-feeling amongst her people, but she did not forego one moment of pleasure on that account, nor swerve a hairsbreadth from the course she had chalked out for herself.

One day, she was sure, women would shake off the foolish antiquated dread of travel and exchange for the dull, inactive and monotonous life which they now led, one in which culture and foreign excursions would incite the mind to study and observation. 'Better to travel and see much, than to live long in ignorance'.

Government House Calcutta

CHAPTER13

RECEPTION AT GOVERNMENT HOUSE AND VISITING THE MARBLE ROCKS OF JUBBLEPORE

On the 23rd January 1877 Dosebai with her son, drove to Government House where she was to be presented to Lady Lytton. On entering the Government House grounds, a gatekeeper showed them where their carriage was to halt, and a footman opened the door and helped her to alight. Indoors, they found everything in the best-appointed style. They were conducted to Lady Burne's apartments where she received them warmly and led them to a suite of rooms furnished with rich, gilded sofas. The doors and windows were hung with splendid, heavily embossed satin curtains. They had not waited long before Lady Lytton made her appearance. She was stately in manners and dress and Dosebai was pleased to see marks of improvement in her health since the first time she had seen her, on her landing in Bombay. She greeted them very cordially and asking them to sit beside her on a sofa, entered into conversation with them about their travels and expressed her admiration of the Parsi ladies' dress and ornaments, especially those Dosebai was wearing on the occasion. Dosebai requested permission to show her the likenesses of her husband Cowasjee and Goolbai, her daughter, inlaid on the cover of her watch and set with diamonds. This was very much admired by the ladies.

Lady Lytton asked Dosebai about her impressions of Calcutta and how long she intended to stay and on hearing that she proposed to leave the very next day, she kindly suggested that it would be well if they could remain a few days longer as on the following 26th she was to hold a reception, where Dosebai could see the guests in their novel *toilettes* – long trained court dresses. She then suggested that Dosebai should make good use of the intervening time by paying a visit to Barrackpore, which was certainly worth a visit. Dosebai appreciated Lady Lytton's kindness, and said that it would give her great pleasure to attend Her ladyship's reception and she would definitely therefore, delay her departure, employing the interval in visiting Barrackpore. After this, they took their leave and while going into the hall in company with Lady Burne, she asked Dosebai if she would send her photograph to Lady Lytton, whereupon Dosebai at once handed her one her son had with him, which Lady Burne took and hastened to deliver to Lady Lytton, who was leaving the hall. She accepted it and said, with a graceful inclination of the head –'This will always remind me of your visit'.

Lady Burne then showed them over Government House and the Reception Hall to initiate them into the ceremonies that Dosebai was so shortly to take part in. She escorted them up the last flight of stairs, and on the landing they met Lady Strachey, to whom they were introduced. At parting, they conveyed their deep sense of appreciation for all these favours to Lady Burne. She and her noble husband were well known for their courtesy and kindness and what they had previously heard about them proved no exaggeration. Such prominent officials did much to promote the peace and interest of the people and strengthen the bonds of the British Empire in India.

After breakfast on the 24th, Dosebai went shopping, and returning at one for lunch, she found two invitation cards for the Reception, but referring her to Mrs. Ezra, who would acquaint her with the forms and etiquette to be observed. As she was no novice in such matters, it seemed unnecessary to trouble her friend. She thought, however, that there might be some difference between the state functions here and at Bombay, so she went to Mrs Ezra and consulted her about the dress she should wear. Mrs Ezra took Dosebai to her dressing-room, where a number of rich, elegant and beautifully embroidered dresses were hanging up, each one of which must have absorbed the cost of a rich gold ornament and a bit more.

On the morning of the 26th, she set to work preparing a dress for the evening's reception, and this was the first time in her travels that she had recourse to the friendly needle, but she made up for the neglect by sewing busily the whole day.

That evening, at half past nine, she and her son entered Government House, and ascending the grand stairs, came upon an imposing spectacle. There was an immense, glittering crowd. In the absence of dear Lady Burne as well as of her Bombay friends, Dosebai was at a loss at what to do in this strange place, but she did not remain long in suspense. She caught sight of Sir Albert Sassoon's family, and in their midst her fears soon vanished. She found, however, much difference between the two Government Houses. At Calcutta, many more ceremonies and formalities were exacted. Firstly, all the guests assembled together in a large hall, after which the gentlemen retired to another room. In the Reception Room, on a dais surmounted by a canopy, stood Lord and Lady Lytton, and as each lady filed past, the Aide-de-camp called out her name and she made her bow by a graceful inclination of her head to their Excellencies, who responded in a similar manner. Later on, the ladies were rejoined by their husbands and sons, who had gone through the same procedure and the rest of the evening was spent in the spacious and brilliantly lit saloons, where the noble hosts moved among their guests, exchanging greetings and a few passing words.

Seeing only one Parsi lady among such a large gathering, there were smiling faces directed towards them. All the ladies present wore most beautiful dresses, but Mrs. Ezra's was the most expensive and Lady Lytton's the most charming – such was the general opinion of Dosebai. There was one noteworthy feature of the dresses on this occasion that was new to her and it was the long trains on the dresses, so that when a lady walked, her dress occupied a considerable amount of space behind her. Here she saw Lady Temple, wife of the Governor of Bombay, who looked extremely pretty and young. Dosibai made many new acquaintances, and all admired her dress. Lady Strachey complimented her by observing, 'Everyone here is pleased by your presence, as you are the first Parsi lady who has come to the Reception Hall at Calcutta.'

Several other ladies asked her name and address for the purpose of paying her a visit but she had to decline the kindness and honour by informing them that after a brief visit to Barrackpore, she would take her departure from Calcutta. Thus she lost the opportunity of making new friends but the pleasure of that evening and the kind interest everyone present seemed to feel for her awoke in her a feeling of joy, which she would cherish all her life.

On the 27th, after an early breakfast, they set out with Bai Sakerbai, her daughters, daughter-in-law and grandchildren for Barrackpore, which they reached by train at about ten o'clock. The first British 'Barrack' or Cantonment was built here in 1772. The sprawling Government Estate and impressive Government House was constructed to provide the Viceroy with a country retreat some fifteen miles outside Calcutta. Having enjoyed a glimpse of this endearing place they returned to Calcutta the same evening. There remained very little time at their disposal to pack up their luggage, preparatory to their departure the next morning. They left their noble host's place at 9 am with every member of his family, except himself, to see them off at the station.

After a continuous journey of two nights and one day, they reached Jubblepore, where they found the manager of Set Muncherjee Pantaky's firm awaiting them at the station and with whom they made their way to Mr. Muncherjee's bungalow, where they received a hearty welcome and a substantial breakfast. Later that morning, they started to view the noteworthy sights of the city and to begin with, they went to see the jail, where the inmates were making good, strong rugs, towels, baskets and other things. The prisoners on the whole looked far from discontented, busily working at their respective employments. This jail was very extensive, being as large as a small village. Visiting the Bazaars and also the British barracks, they went to the public gardens, which were very famous for roses. In variety, size and fragrance, they were far superior to any Dosebai had ever seen. On their return home they arranged to start early the next morning to see the famous marble rocks and accordingly, retired to rest in good time.

By break of day on the 30th they set out in the cool morning air and by a circuitous route, reached a hill at 7 am. They halted there for their man to prepare tea and then sat down to a comfortable breakfast that they had brought with them (one did it in style). It was most delightful to sit here and enjoy the beauties of nature. Duly fortified, they set out walking up the hill and soon came to the ruins of a temple, celebrated for having contained no fewer than sixty-five idols. Climbing further up, they could hear the famous waterfall long before they saw it and were stunned by the deafening noise caused by the tremendous rush of water. It was fascinating to see such a huge quantity of water continually flowing with such force day and night. The source of this cascade was way up in these hills and further down, the river was wide and navigable. Hiring a boat, they went for a sail on the river, the better to view the scenery. The rising rocks on either side were all of marble, for the most part white, but interspersed with blocks of black and brown. The river meandered through and around them in the most fantastic manner. It widened into a broad basin, like a large lake, surrounded by hills about a thousand feet in height. The scenery all along was breath taking as the marble rocks assumed the appearance of palaces rising sheer out of the water. Her old aunty, lost in utter amazement, would point to these and exclaim; 'Are these abodes of humans or ethereal beings?'

On the 31st January, they left Jubblepore at 9 am and after travelling for twenty-four hours, they steamed into Byculla Station in Bombay where Dosebai soon spotted her dear husband, daughter and youngest son waiting for them. She offered up her thanks to the Almighty for seeing them all in good health, as well as for the happy termination of her Indian tour.

In conclusion, she mentioned again the Delhi Durbar, which was so indelibly fixed in her memory. Here, in her own words, is what she wrote: 'Such a sight must have been extremely noble to all present, for, though the pomp and pageantry of Royal State is not unknown in England, the sombre garments of black which prevail there must make such scenes dull and uninteresting; whereas the different nationalities represented at Delhi on this occasion, the thousand varieties of dress they wore and the magnificent jewels of

95

the native princes rendered the Imperial Durbar one of the most brilliant and unique spectacles that the nineteenth century has ever witnessed.'

CHAPTER 14

LORD LYTTON AT GANESH KHIND
AND
ANOTHER VISIT TO CALCUTTA

The Durbar at Delhi proved a source of countless blessings to the poor by opening up new industries, while the circulation of wealth effected by the progress of so many Rajahs through the land as well as by the magnificent preparations made by the Government, served to lessen to some extent the horrors of famine locally. Moreover, the Princes too, confined till now to their respective territories, must have gained an insight into the order and enlightenment of English rule and thereby laid up a fund of experience and knowledge from their travels to and from Delhi.

After Dosebai's return home, she soon resumed her domestic duties and particularly the management of a small garden in which the greater portion of her day was spent. Notwithstanding this, she never neglected to take an evening walk or drive, not even once, for from her early days she knew the advantages of exercise.

An Exhibition was to be held in Poona, so Dosebai decided to go. On arriving at the Exhibition building, she found a guard of honour drawn up near the entrance and troops ranged on both the sides, and then she heard that Lord Lytton, being in Poona, was to grace the Exhibition with his presence. Several influential Parsi gentlemen who had come there asked her if she had dropped in at that time for the express purpose of seeing the Viceroy. She affirmed that she had not the remotest idea of the Viceroy's being there until she entered the building. In due course, Lord Lytton arrived and everyone stood up to do him honour.

Dosebai was seated on a couch in a remote corner and on the Viceroy's walking around to look at the pictures he recognised her, and after shaking hands with her, asked if she was a resident of Poona. She replied that she had come up from Bombay where she usually resided, the day before and expressed her pleasure at this unexpected meeting. Her friend, Col. O. T. Burne was also there and hoped to see her the next day at the Government House party. When she enquired after the health of Lady Lytton and Mrs. Burne, she was informed that they were well and always remembered her. It was thought by the bystanders that His Excellency Lord Lytton had, out of mere courtesy, shaken hands and spoken with her, and His Excellency Sir Richard Temple, the then newly appointed Governor of Bombay, entertained the same notion, but it came to be subsequently known that prior to this, she had been a guest at Government House, Calcutta.

Early on the morning of 25th August, an invitation for the party to be held at Government House that day was sent to her. Dosebai would have been around forty-five years of age at this time. As neither her husband nor her son were in Poona, she asked Lady Sassoon to accompany her, so they drove together to Ganesh Khind in the afternoon. Although she had taken part in many such entertainments in Bombay, this was her first visit to the Government House at Poona, and its relaxed and friendly ambiance struck her forcibly. His Excellency Lord Lytton mixed freely with his guests, shaking hands with the ladies. He entered into conversation with her. The company dispersed themselves about the beautiful gardens and the scene was a pretty picture of social enjoyment. She returned home at seven in the evening and from this day forth, her name was enrolled amongst the guests at Ganesh Khind, the Government House of Poona.

Soon after this party, Lord Lytton left for Madras (now Chenai), to set on foot means for alleviating the sufferings of the famine stricken population there and this humane action endeared him to all. Dosebai remained longer than usual in Poona on this occasion, enjoying the pleasures of the season. She had not omitted to bring her own carriage and horses, and in addition, she bought a handsome pair of ponies and a Park phaeton, which she used to drive herself, enjoying a drive both morning and evening. On 21st September, Lord Lytton returned from Madras and received an enthusiastic welcome. His Lordship and Sir O. Burne caught sight of her and returned her salaams by raising their hats. This did not fail to draw the attention of their officers who looked towards her with smiling faces. (It's that Parsi lady, again)!

There was to be a ball at Government House that evening, for which she had duly received an invitation, but having no one else to accompany her, she had written to ask if she might bring her youngest son of twelve with her. The answer to this was in the affirmative, so they left at nine o'clock for Ganesh Khind. It was beautifully illuminated and every nook and cranny in the garden was lit up. Captain Anderson escorted them to the Ballroom where dancing had commenced. She was late, and felt a little embarrassed, but Mrs Rivett-Carnac, wife of the Military Secretary to His Excellency Sir R. Temple, came up and drew her to a sofa beside her and put her at ease. She met many of her English friends and conversed with their Excellencies Lord Lytton and Sir R. Temple and with Sir O.T. Burne, Ladies Staveley and Sassoon, Mrs Gibbs and others who were all glad to see her there. I am not at all sure what her twelve-year-old son made of it all.

It was two hours past midnight when, having thoroughly enjoyed this exquisite and refined entertainment, she rose to depart, on seeing which, the good Governor asked Captain Anderson to escort her to her carriage. She thanked him for his civility. It was three o'clock when she finally retired to rest. At this ball, she was several times asked by gentlemen to dance but had to excuse herself, never having learnt this graceful accomplishment.

On her return to Bombay she found that during her absence, everything at home had been neglected and so she had to labour afresh to restore order and harmony. Her dear husband was too occupied with business affairs to notice what was going on in the house.

One morning, she read in the papers that an Exhibition would be held at Paris in 1878. From her very infancy her imagination, stimulated by Col. Jarvis' vivid descriptions, had pictured in fascinating colours the pomp and charm of England, and she had always entertained the hope of one day being able to visit it. Her childish dream had been that soon after her marriage her husband and she should go to England but reality proved this to be impracticable. But now, comparatively late in life, it seemed as if her hopes were to be fulfilled. Although her husband's business affairs would not allow his absence from Bombay, he joyfully assented to her going.

In the year 1866, when her daughter was in England and in the family way, she had resolved to go out to her, but had been compelled to abandon the idea, as Cowasjee could not accompany her and her eldest son was not of an age to do so. This son was now grown up, and the opening of the Paris Exhibition furnished a good occasion for the long wished for voyage. Her daughter was now back in Bombay, and Dosebai felt no hesitation in leaving her husband and younger son. With his father's consent, the eldest son was to accompany her. Her brother, from the kindest of intentions, offered to apprise his friends in England of her coming and request them, and in particular Mr. Leith (of Messrs. Forbes and Co), to give her a welcome and render what assistance they could. Mr Leith had frequently seen Dosebai moving in English society in Bombay, and had remarked to her brother that she was the only Parsi lady who did so. Her brother also asked for her photograph for the purpose of enclosing it in his letter.

During the following month, she was engaged in making preparations for her long and perilous journey. Warm clothing was made up and all requisites gathered together. Her next job was to settle some monetary affairs between herself and her eldest brother Dorabjee, who lived in Calcutta and she made up her mind to revisit that place.

On the 8th of March Dosebai left Bombay with her youngest son and safely reached Calcutta on the morning of the 11th. She took up

100

residence with her brother at Garden Reach, a most fashionable part of town. She saw her worthy friend, Bai Sakerbai, who was much surprised to see her, and also had the pleasure of seeing her friend Lady Sassoon, at her daughter Mrs. Ezra's place, and both mother and daughter were much interested on hearing of Dosebai's intended voyage to England, which Mrs. Ezra said was certainly worth seeing.

Her friends enquired if she had waited upon Lady Lytton. But as Her Ladyship stayed at Barrackpore, she could not do so during her limited stay at Calcutta. Young Mrs. Ezra had placed her splendid carriage at Dosebai's disposal and she made use of it on every important occasion during her stay. Hearing on the 12th from Bai Sakerbai that Lady Lytton had returned to Calcutta that very day, she wrote to ask if Her ladyship would make it convenient to see her.

On the 13th she opened the subject of her visit to England to her brother, and he at once consented to pay her all her dues. In the evening, she drove in a handsome open carriage to the fashionable resort of the city, where she had driven in a closed carriage a year before. She, being the first Parsi lady to drive in an open carriage, formed the object of general attraction. Their Excellencies, Lord and Lady Lytton drove past her, and at once recognising, bowed to her, which showed that her interview with Their Excellencies still lived in their memory. On her return to her brother's house, she found that a note had been left for her, by a messenger, to the effect that Her Excellency Lady Lytton would be glad to see her the next day.

On the 14th afternoon Dosebai went, with her son, to Government House and met with a cordial reception by Lady Lytton. She expressed her approval of the intended visit to England. Her Ladyship noticed the cap worn by her son, which was set round with family portraits, and was surprised to hear that the handsome and intricate embellishment was Dosebai's own handiwork. Her Ladyship told her that she had preserved the photo, received a year ago, and Dosebai on her side, expressed her acknowledgements for the favour done her. She respectfully enquired if Lady Lytton would condescend to accept from her, a cap similarly embroidered to that of her son. 'If it is costly,' she replied, ' I regret I cannot'. But when

Dosebai said that her labour was all its value, in addition to some small pearls used merely to enhance the effect of the needlework, Her Ladyship did her the favour of accepting the same, and ordered an officer, who was in waiting, to go and fetch the box containing the cap from the carriage. On seeing the cap, which was found to be as represented by Dosebai, far from costly, Her Ladyship admired it and thanked her for her humble gift. In the crown, a portrait of Lord Lytton, her illustrious husband, was set, which pleased Her Ladyship the most.

With Lady Lytton's praise of her needlework and her hearty good wishes for a safe voyage to the shores of her homeland, Dosebai took her leave, happy and excited. After lunch, she went to her brother's place, got all her packing done, and with her luggage went back to her friend's. While they were sitting together, a mounted *sowar* came to deliver a box and a note to her from Government House. The former contained a photograph of Lady Lytton in an ornamental ormolu frame bearing her monogram and crest. It was much admired by all her friends and she penned her grateful acknowledgement for this fresh mark of Her Ladyship's kindness to her.

Her visit to Calcutta had been more advantageous than she had anticipated. She had met lady Sassoon and her daughter, enjoyed an unexpected interview with Lady Lytton, and her brother had paid her back the money loan.

She secured a passage for herself and her elder son, in a steamer leaving from Bombay on the 31st of May 1878. Their names were in the newspaper of the day as passengers on the *S.S. Nizam*.

Her husband and youngest son kept them company as far as Apollo Bunder, where they bade each other a temporary farewell. Here many of her friends had assembled to wish them Bon Voyage. The steamer weighed anchor at five o'clock. The sea was serene, a delightful breeze fanned the sails, and Dosebai's lifelong, dearly cherished hope of seeing England was soon to be realised.

CHAPTER 15

ON THE S.S. NIZAM

On the very first day on board, Dosebai made the acquaintance of three people whose kindness and attention lasted throughout the voyage. They were Mr. James, Postmaster General of Bombay and Major and Mrs. Mathew. The time on the steamer passed most pleasantly and the sea, thank goodness, had no evil effects on them. Her son-in-law as well as other friends had in jest, painted gloomy pictures of the troubles they would have to encounter as war was declared between Russia and Turkey. They laughingly said that Dadabhoy and she would have to fight on one side or another, provided they escaped alive from the tempests that prevailed during this season on the way to England; but of all this they experienced nothing.

They reached Aden on 7th June at 7 am, and all the passengers were in a hurry to get ashore. To their surprise, some men in the employ of Mr Cowasjee Dinshawjee Adenwalla came on board and politely requested the two of them to take their seats in the boat sent for them by their boss, who would be glad to see them. They accordingly seated themselves in the boat, were pulled quickly to shore and escorted to the residence and store of Mr Cowasjee. The two brothers, Messrs Cowasjee and Dorabjee, putting business aside, came out and cordially shaking hands, welcomed them to their house. 'We did not know of your coming,' they said, 'or we should have come on board to welcome you ourselves'. Thus it transpired that the employees, recognising them as Parsis, had invited them in their master's name, knowing full well that it would please him. They refreshed themselves with a hot bath and breakfast and after a lapse of seven days on board the ship, they again enjoyed dishes cooked in the Parsi fashion. After this, they took their seats in a carriage and pair which was waiting for them and, accompanied by the son of their host and his manager, they had a long drive and saw a great deal of the city of Aden and its neighbourhood.

Returning later to the airy and commodious quarters of their host, they sat down to pen letters to their Bombay friends and relatives, telling them of their safe arrival so far, and of the handsome welcome accorded to them by their neighbours (for the Adenwalla family occupied the bungalow adjoining theirs in Bombay).

At dinner, they heard that Admiral Sir John Corbett with his Troopship was then at Aden. On the previous day he had paid a visit to Mr. Cowasjee and had spoken of Dosebai's friendship with him. He would have been much pleased to see her here, but there was no time for a call on him. After cordially thanking Messrs Cowasjee and Dorabjee they were escorted back to the steamer at three o'clock, sailing away an hour later. Among the passengers was a Hindu gentleman named Shivnath, a brother of the Rajah of Oude. He was bound for England where, under the guardianship of Mr. Fitzgerald, he was to receive a sound English education. The young gentleman was good-natured and amiable and consequently a friendship sprang up between him and Dosebai's son, so that he was very much in their company. There were some amateur musicians, singers and instrumentalists amongst the passengers on board, who enthusiastically enlivened the tedium with their performances. The Captain was very genial and the Red Sea was crossed amidst much merriment and pleasure.

One night, a short but entertaining drama was performed and every day brought with it some new amusement. On the 12th June, at about noon, they anchored off Suez and some of the most gifted musicians left them, to continue their journey via Brindisi. At 3 pm the S.S. NIzam entered the Suez Canal which, being very shallow, necessitated a very slow progress. (The Suez Canal was opened in 1869, only nine years earlier). At sunset they came to a standstill, remaining stationary the whole night and resuming their slow progress the next morning through scenery devoid of interest or variety. On the 13th they reached Port Said, in Egypt, and went on shore to see the place. It was an unpretentious little town, and only came into being thanks to the construction of the Suez Canal. A newcomer could not fail to be struck by a novel feature of locomotion. The people here rode on mules of such pygmy size that the rider's legs touched the ground. They could not help laughing heartily at this ludicrous sight. Small coffee bars were dotted about the streets and to Dosebai's amazement, there were girls singing and dancing in them. In one of these places, Dosebai ordered a cup of coffee but it was so bitter as to be most unpalatable. The novelty of her costume created much curiosity and quite a mob gathered round them, saying that they had never seen such a dress before.

On the 17th afternoon they reached Malta and their steamer steered deftly through the narrow alleys formed by a number of ships and sailing craft of all sorts, finally coming to a halt. This being the time of the Russo-Turkish War, Indian forces were mustered in Malta in large numbers and the harbour was very busy. Dosebai and Dadabhoy, along with their fellow passenger Mr. Shivnath, hired a boat and went on shore. After ascending a flight of stone steps, they came upon a gateway, such as is generally seen in large fortresses. This led to another flight of steps, which led them up to the main road. Here they hired a light, open carriage. The fares of these public conveyances were regulated according to the length of time the vehicle is occupied. (This taxi concept would have been quite novel to Dosebai).

His Royal Highness the Duke of Cambridge, Commander-in-Chief of the British Army, was this day to hold a grand Review of the Indian Troops. This imposing display of the British forces, fortunately for them, was to take place the day they landed at Malta. The ground selected for the manoeuvres was surrounded by big, stately buildings and every window and balcony of these houses was crowded to an excess. All available open space around was occupied fully by spectators on foot or in carriages. To obtain a better view, they left their conveyance and shortly after his Royal Highness, in full uniform and mounted on a splendid black charger, rode up. Standing here she soon attracted attention; from her dress some guessed that she came from India, and others, from China. She was seen and recognised by Mrs. Hunter, wife of Dr. Hunter of Bombay, who came up to her and introduced her to the lady who was with her, Mrs Beattie, wife of Surgeon-General Beattie of Bombay.

The next day the steamer weighed anchor. As they left, the town of Malta looked very picturesque in the afternoon sun and gradually receded from view as they left the shores far behind. Reading, the writing of her travel diary and the agreeable company on board the steamer made the time pass most pleasantly.

Early on the morning of the 22nd of June they reached Gibraltar. It looked like a marble mountain split into two. Again, they hired a conveyance and set out to see the town. The long, winding road took them up the hill and to the recreation park, which commanded a fine view. Proceeding further they came to the Spanish frontier. The most remarkable feature of Gibraltar was the turning of the natural summit of the mountain into a castellated fortress, mounted in every nook and corner with heavy guns. A large garrison of British troops was permanently stationed at this strategic outpost. In the course of four hours they had seen all that there was to be seen and returning to the steamer at ten o'clock, they left the port. Viewed from the sea, Gibraltar looked like a forbidding mountain rising straight up from the ocean.

On the evening of the 26th, their journey being about to terminate, one of the passengers proposed a vote of thanks to their worthy commander, Captain Barlow.

On the 27th June, by the glimmer of an early dawn, they saw the indistinct outline of Southampton and shortly after, the steamer dropped anchor. Letters were brought to them from land; amongst these was one from Mr. Dadabhoy, formerly in the employ of her husband and now living in London, asking her to telegraph him as soon as she arrived in Southampton, so that he might meet them on alighting at London. They could now plainly see the celebrated and impressive Netley Hospital, built in 1856 and having the accolade of being the world's longest building at the time. It was a military hospital very much in use from the days of Florence Nightingale right up to the Second World War but finally demolished in 1966. At

107

six o'clock the steamer started again and within an hour had entered the Dock at Southampton and taken up her position near the wharf. All were soon busily engaged in looking after their luggage, and after bidding 'Goodbye' to their able Captain, they left the ship and took themselves off to the Custom House nearby.

When the officials came to inspect their luggage, they looked at Dosebai with curiosity. She said to them, 'I am no merchant, I have no cigars or tobacco with me. You are, however, at liberty to inspect my packages, but pray, do not detain us unnecessarily, I have come here only to see the Paris Exhibition.' On hearing this, they readily allowed the luggage to pass and also asked her not to go out in the streets of London with such a profusion of jewellery upon her person. From here they went to a large Railway station. There were fruit and confectioners' stalls at the station at which pretty girls were employed as saleswomen, and an interminable crowd of people kept coming and going at all the doors. She records with delight that the name of Sir Jamsetjee Jeejeebhoy, the Parsi philanthropist, was well known out here too, and when she said that she was a Parsi, she was at once identified as being of the same race as Sir Jamsetjee. During the whole journey and throughout her stay in England, she wore her usual Parsi costume. Five or six Parsi ladies had been in England before her, her own daughter amongst them, but none of them continued to wear their native dresses without making many changes and modifications even when at home, whilst in public they appeared only in English dress, but she went everywhere in her Parsi dress and was, in consequence, very much spoken of. Everybody was anxious to see her on account of the peculiarity of her dress, and her appearance was evidently, as novel and interesting to them as theirs was to her.

On the railway journey to London they felt it as warm as in Bombay. The green landscape of England was very beautiful and wherever the train stopped, crowds of people were to be seen. They passed well-built houses and tall smoky factory chimneys and away in the distance, they saw hills and fields of grass – all so very new and pleasant to their eyes as to beggar description. The rugged, gnarled trunks of great trees, like ivy-bound pillars, the leafy avenues, the open meadows, the rich, velvety grass spun by Nature's own hands, and the cooling green foliage were all new sights to Dosebai. Excepting the slight smoke of the engine, they did not experience the least inconvenience either of dust or noise. A neat, little, thatched cottage, enveloped in a profusion of flowering creepers was a novel, picturesque and charming sight. As they drew near the great metropolis, rows of stately buildings came into view and soon the grand panorama of London, with an immense wilderness of chimneys emitting thick, black smoke, burst upon their astounded gaze. The network of railway lines intersecting and running into each other and the grand and majestic bridge over the Thames amazed them. Here, at Waterloo Bridge Station, she set foot at last in London, and the great aim of her life was realised.

CHAPTER 16

IN THE CAPITAL OF THE BRITISH EMPIRE 1878

The train arrived at Waterloo Bridge Station where she was surprised to see great crowds of people, though nothing unusual was going on as far as she could make out. (Not much change there, then)! With mutual good wishes, they took leave of their fellow passengers who had accompanied them thus far, and entering a horse-drawn cab, drove to the house of Mr. Dadabhoy, alias Dady, Solicitor, in Fitzroy Square. After waiting in vain for their telegram, this gentleman had gone out, but they were welcomed by his wife and her maid, who came out to the cab and begged them to alight as Mr. Dady was expected back shortly. After a refreshing cup of tea they felt rested and shortly after, Mr. Dady came in and greeted them most cordially. He had not rented any lodgings for them beforehand, as he thought it better for her to select one herself. Accordingly, Dosebai accompanied him in a cab and saw some apartments that were to be let but did not find any to her taste. Then, they drove to Cavendish Street, Portland Place, where at No.23 she found well-furnished apartments, in a central location - just the thing she wanted. The landlord, Mr. Baker, was an old man. His grown-up daughter lived with him and managed the house. Mr. Dady settled the rent with them, after which she returned with him and rested for the night at his house.

The next morning, they removed to the newly-hired lodgings, and Mrs. Dady's maid took Dosebai to one of the grand public baths, situated at a distance of a mile or so from their lodgings, for in London all houses did not have this most necessary adjunct. These bathing places were splendid edifices and were divided into separate compartments. Each compartment was furnished with a large tub, hot and cold water, towels and a mirror. There were also maidservants there to assist the ladies. Turkish baths could also be had here but the charges, comparatively, were a little higher. After taking a bath, she returned to Mr. Dady's and dined there in Parsi fashion, as she was quite bored with the European food she had during the long voyage.

In the evening, Mr. Dady took them to Madame Tussaud's Waxworks. They entered a large hall fitted up like a palace and brilliantly illuminated. Here they saw arranged in groups, wax figures reclining on rich sofas or standing under a canopy representing in the most life-like manner, the rulers of different nations surrounded by their families and nobilities, all superbly clad in their respective costumes. Art had so closely imitated nature that it was often difficult to distinguish the living from the waxen figures. One waxen figure of an old man, with a snuffbox in his hand offering a pinch to the passers-by, was such a clever imitation that many an onlooker was deceived. On the other hand, visitors themselves were often mistaken for the waxen exhibits. They were much attracted by the sight of an exceedingly stout lady seated on a divan in the midst of a group of waxen figures; her remarkable corpulence, her rigid attitude and her fixed stare of surprise, drew towards her the attention of a young man who accompanied them. Noticing that her eyelids moved, as he thought, by some clever mechanism, he approached, as he thought, the waxen figure with the intention of touching the eyeballs, when the supposed figure stood up indignantly, to the wonder and merriment of all.

One room contained an exact representation of a court of justice and another the death scene of a nihilist about to suffer on the scaffold and a third showed how captive kings bewailed their cruel lot in such woebegone attitudes and expressions, that they felt quite sorry for them At the time of their visit, Pope Pius IX had recently died, and his death scene was portrayed with terrible realism. Dosebai was fascinated with all they saw here and it was past eleven before they returned home. Hearing that a flower show of every known species of the rose was to be held the next day at the renowned Crystal Palace, she arranged with Mr. Dady to go there, so, early on the following day, Mrs Dady, her maid, Dosebai and her son started by railway from Victoria Station for this wonderfully beautiful place.

So huge was the crowd there, that Dosebai, being in her native dress and having several ornaments on, was quite wary. The railway here was conveniently constructed to lead right into the Crystal Palace Park, whence a flight of wooden stairs ushered the visitor into the main building. Having been kindly but firmly warned that her dress and jewels would attract attention, she kept close to her son on the right side and the maidservant on the left. She heard one remark in the crowd that the Rose Show, being an annual event, was not so great an attraction as was her picturesque dress. Some of the gentlemen there were pleased to find her able to converse with them in their own tongue and consequently, she felt herself quite at home in their company.

A scene akin to one from fairyland burst upon her astonished gaze when they reached the top of the stairs. Standing on a balcony as broad as a public thoroughfare, she could see nothing but a continuous and most beautifully laid out garden, in the midst of which stood the glittering palace on raised ground. As the name indicates, the Crystal Palace was a superb palace of glass, that is to say, its roof, ceiling and floors were all constructed of glass. Pieces of thick glass set in iron frames were used in building this most elegant and fantastic masterpiece. Instigated by Prince Albert and designed by Sir Joseph Paxton, it was built in 1851 to house the Great Exhibition. The technique of making plate glass had just been perfected. The Crystal Palace occupied a commanding position and was divided into a number of courts, picture galleries and a museum. The wonderfully colourful and fragrant show of roses collected together in the spacious hall was indescribably beautiful. Countless varieties of roses, all in the perfection of cultivation, were so artistically arranged that one never tired of admiring them.

When fatigued with walking, they entered a refreshment area and then headed towards the picture gallery, as she had been told that it contained a portrait of her daughter, Goolbai, done when she was in England in 1868. It was impossible to praise this most excellent collection enough. The walls, throughout their full length, were hung with pictures drawn by celebrated artists, representing in life-like reality kings, queens, peasants, beggars, giants, fairies and scenes from nature. All these paintings she saw with ever-increasing wonder; some of them were so rare and quite priceless. As the afternoon wore on, the crowd began to increase and at five the Lord Mayor of London and his retinue honoured the show with their presence. The Lord Mayor, Sir Charles Whetham, was of a good and noble appearance and elicited remarks of homage and respect from the people.

They next visited the Egyptian and other courts and saw there the effigies of the various lands, but although the whole day was spent in the Crystal Palace, there was much within left unseen, while they had not visited the gardens at all. They therefore strolled out and the sight of the splendid garden at the still hour of dusk, with its lovely flowerbeds and fountains was extremely pleasant, but as Dosebai was informed that there were many more lovely gardens in London, she did not linger here. There were athletic sports going on which were, to say the least, wonderful to watch. From here, they took leave of the sparkling Crystal Palace.

On the 1st of July she hired a cab and set out to see the public gardens, the principal one being Hyde Park. Her acquaintances warned her, again, not to wear jewellery for, mingling with the good and harmless society, were light fingered gentry of both sexes, so well attired as to defy detection. From this place, she returned home through Regent's Park and resolved to pass all her leisure hours during her stay in London amidst the beautiful surroundings of Hyde Park.

On the 2nd she went for a carriage drive through Oxford and Regent Streets, Piccadilly and Bond Street. On returning to her lodgings, she was gladdened by receiving letters from Bombay. That afternoon, they took a drive along the embankment of the Thames, where a gentle breeze playing on the glass-like surface of the river and the sight of several magnificent bridges soothed their spirits. In Dosebai's words, 'One of the characteristic features of London is its capacity for dispelling care and sadness; no-one, however careworn and depressed can resist its joyful influence.'

Later that day, they went to the London Polytechnic, where they saw the latest inventions and wonderfully modern machines. They even saw a Telephone and panoramic pictures of the Paris Exhibition and of several battlefields. Her son paid a visit to Sir O. T. Burne, who was very pleased to see him and gave him much useful information and advice.

On the 3rd July, Dosebai set out to purchase some fancy articles and went in search of a jeweller who had, seventeen years previously, supplied her with ornaments and jewellery. His name was Webb and she was not long in finding out his establishment. He was glad to see his own work again after so many years and which, he said, was still fashionable. He praised her refined taste and said he would be glad to execute further orders from her. She visited other jewellers' shops too. All of these shops appeared to her so rich and splendid that it made it difficult to choose one over another. On learning that Parisian jewellery was of finer and more elaborate workmanship, she ordered a limited number of old ornaments to be remodelled according to the prevailing fashion, and deferred her purchases until she went to France. Quitting the shops, she drove past Buckingham Palace to Hyde Park, where she remained but a short time on account of the cold. The following day several jewellers called upon her, and much of the day was spent in showing and drawing new patterns and designs.

When she went out for a walk the next evening, seeing a number of beautiful girls alight from every horse-drawn omnibus, she asked them if they were all coming from school, when they laughingly replied that they were shop girls. In the large shops hundreds of girls were employed as salesgirls and seamstresses. The idea of women working in commerce and earning a living was most unusual and impressive for Dosebai. While walking along, she met Mr. Stevens, who, with his wife and daughter, was on his way to pay her a visit. This gentleman was the senior partner in the firm of Forbes and Co., and although he was well acquainted with the people of India, his wife and daughter, who had never been to India, were not and they were therefore rather interested in Dosebai and invited her to a tea party at their house.

Next on the tourist list was Westminster Hall and the Abbey. Passing through Trafalgar Square, where there was a high monument erected to the great Naval Commander Horatio Nelson, they came to a very large and stately building. This building was divided into many departments, such as the Tower Court and the Houses of Parliament. Here, she saw the splendid throne used by Queen Victoria when she came to open Parliament. To the left of this was the Prince Consort's throne, which unhappily, had been unoccupied for several years. After spending four hours wandering round these magnificent buildings they went to see Westminster Abbey. Its spacious compound was used as a graveyard for the celebrated and worthy of the land. The priest in charge of this Abbey kindly explained to her all the rites and ceremonies of Christian burial and pointed out some very fine monuments with elaborate and exquisite sculpture. The colossal hall of this fine abbey branched off like a public thoroughfare, into four different sections and was capable of accommodating thousands at a time.

On the 7th July she received visits from Sir. Burne and other friends and in the afternoon, she went, with her son, to Mrs. Stevens' party at their residence in Upper Phillimore Gardens. A visit to the Kensington Gardens terminated the rambles of the day.

The next day, the Royal Horticultural Society were holding a Flower and Fruit Show at the Westminster Halls, so she went along to see it, and found it well worth a visit. The Royal family and many of the nobility were also there. On the following day, Dosebai went to see the Royal Aquarium, but as she was there before opening time, she had to wait beside the Westminster Hospital. A gentleman came up and politely requested her to take a seat in one of the rooms of the hospital. She gladly availed herself of this opportunity, and was no sooner seated there than an elderly lady who, she afterwards learnt, was the matron, came into the room and asked if she would like to go over the Hospital. The arrangements inside were admirable and interested her extremely. The Hospital was a large, many storeyed building and she was so tired by the time she had looked over the first two floors, that she was about to retire, when the matron pressingly requested her to go over the whole building to satisfy the curiosity of its inmates; for, she assured Dosebai, that no foreign lady in such a costume as hers had ever been seen in the whole of England before! Moreover, she added, the patients were cheered by the kindness she showed them. She could not but comply with this request, and was thanked by many for the trouble she took. Before leaving, the matron very kindly invited her to have some refreshments, which she politely declined, as she had eaten breakfast not long before.

They then went to the Aquarium, which to Dosebai, presented an unusual and picturesque appearance. It appeared as if a river was dammed up by glass and parcelled out into different compartments with glass all around. The bed of this artificial river was strewn with shells, sand and seaweed. Swimming about hither and thither were fish of all sizes, colours and description. She had never seen such a sight before. The aquarium was so large that a single day did not suffice to see it all thoroughly. Thus, Dosebai thought, England afforded her people an unceasing round of refined and legitimate pleasures, even a tenth of which could not be had in India. All this, in Dosebai's words, was due to their 'enlightened rulers who, by such unique and marvellous shows, render their country a fairyland full of wonder, beauty, skill and intelligence'.

The Tower of London came next on the agenda. To start with, they saw the Crown Jewels and the valuable silver-wrought ornaments of former kings. The crowns were richly decorated with brilliant rubies and emeralds. Here was also to be seen an excellent imitation of the famous Kohinoor Diamond, the original being worn by the Queen Empress in her crown. Their guide gave them a comprehensive account of all they saw. The next visit was to St. Paul's Cathedral, the largest of its kind in England. She could not say enough in praise of its stately and imposing grandeur and chaste yet elaborate decorations. Led on by a desire to see everything, she climbed up to the Golden Gallery, which was 350 feet from the ground, and was rewarded for her exertions by the wonderful spectacle of London spread out before her. From this height, London looked much like a toy village. Delighted with their visit, they returned home and went at 5 o'clock to Miss Hill's party at Hampstead Heath.

About thirty persons had already assembled and were awaiting her arrival. They gave her a most hearty welcome and began to express their views of her dress and ornaments. She had been requested to bring with her the cap, decorated with her family photographs and was much complimented by the assembly on her exquisite work and designs. The Hill sisters, hostesses of the day had out of filial love, undertaken to write a biography of their worthy father; on hearing this Dosebai informed them that she, too, was engaged in writing her autobiography.

On 15th July, she went to Miss Manning's where she had the pleasure of meeting several Parsis, Muslims and Bengalees. On returning home she found that Mr. Fitzgerald, son of the ex-Governor of Bombay, had called on her, and being most disappointed at having missed him, she wrote to ask him when it would be convenient for him to see them, and the next day he invited them to come at 2 pm, to his residence in Queen's Road, Kensington. They were late, (this, unfortunately, was an Indian tendency), and Mr. Fitzgerald, after waiting a long time for their arrival, had left and they were requested to follow him to Charing Cross Station. The streets round the station were crowded with spectators, and although no other carriages were allowed to enter so late, theirs was at once admitted under Mr. Fitzgerald's instructions.

The Premier, Lord Beaconsfield, and Lord Salisbury were returning home victorious that day from the Berlin Congress, having established peace in Europe without bloodshed and having reconciled two discordant nations, Russia and Turkey, with no other weapon than 'Moral Suasion'. To welcome back these great diplomatic statesmen, the crowds filled the streets.

Charing Cross Station was tastefully decorated with flowers and laurel leaves and everyone seemed to vie with the other in the desire to show honour to England's respected representatives. Inside the station a stand was erected for the accommodation of visitors, where

117

seats in the first row were reserved for Dosebai and her son. At five o'clock the train steamed into the station, when the whole assemblage of spectators rose up to show their respect and there was cheering and waving of hats and handkerchiefs as the two noblemen alighted. To her eyes, both statesmen looked possessed of superior intelligence; they looked what they were – acute politicians and leaders of men. They acknowledged the honour done them by saluting the people in return and entering their carriages, which had driven straight into the station, drove away.

This was the first reception of this kind she had seen in England and it truly impressed her by its very heartiness. People made many a guess as to her nationality; some said she was a Parsi Queen, others an Indian Princess and, as ever, some went so far as to surmise that she was a Chinese lady. Her carriage was literally hemmed in by the crowd, from which it was extricated by two mounted policemen who came to their aid, conducting their carriage through the living mass until it was left behind.

On 17th July Dosebai went to a photographer's, whose establishment seemed to be on a grand scale and largely patronised by the nobility. One of the saloons was reserved for the Royal family. The photographer requested her to return in a couple of days in one of her best costumes, when he would take her portrait and enlarge it to any size she liked. He further begged her to allow him to take a full-sized photograph for himself. This day was Dadabhoy's birthday; and therefore, the day was spent in merriment in the company of their Parsi friends. In the afternoon they went for a drive, spent the evening in Hyde Park and returned home for an extra-special supper.

CHAPTER 17

MEETING MRS. GLADSTONE
AND
A VISIT TO WINDSOR CASTLE

On 18th July 1878, they were invited, by the kind recommendation of Sir Burne, to see the India office. Sir George Birdwood received them cordially and showed them all over the premises. The India Office was a very ornate and elegant building and of so big a size that they could not see more than half of it that day. The elaborate masonry and the statues of Indian worthies with which the frontage is embellished, render this office one of the finest buildings in London and a princely sum must have been spent on its construction. All business connected with India had to go through the India Office. Sir Birdwood asked Dosebai whether she knew Sir Cowasjee Jehangir Readymoney, and was pleased to hear that she was closely related to him.

Next, they drove to the house of Mrs. Wester Phillips and afterwards visited the Zoological Garden, which was not far from there. On the 19th Dosebai went to see Buckingham Palace, for which Mr. Fitzgerald had kindly sent her a card of admission. The beauty of this palace can well be imagined from the fact that it was the residence of the Royal family. The beautiful drawing rooms, the furniture of exquisite workmanship, the rich curtains and carpets and the paintings, executed by master hands all defied description. Needless to say, she was overawed by the royal splendour of this palace. She felt that no one, however morose and melancholy they might be, could see this palace without their spirits being lifted.

On the 20th, she visited Kensington Museum (later to be known as the Victoria and Albert Museum), and on entering the precinct, she saw a statue of her uncle, Sir Cowasjee Jehangir Readymoney, occupying pride of place. He was a leading Parsi industrialist and philanthropist, having contributed millions in charity to build schools, colleges and hospitals in British India. The Parsis originally did not have surnames, as such. They simply adopted their father's first name. In the late 1700s, under British influence, they gave themselves proper surnames, which usually corresponded to their trade. There are therefore several Coopers, Watchmakers, Constables and other English surnames as well as Readymoney (Philanthropist) and many more unusual ones amongst the Parsis.

When she reached home, a messenger from Mr. Dadabhoy came to enquire whether she would go to the Covent Garden Theatre that evening to hear the most famous singer in the world – Madame Patti. She agreed to this proposal and after supper, drove to the theatre. It was a very large theatre, capable of seating several hundred persons. Madame Patti played her part excellently. Her singing being in Italian elicited great applause from those who were conversant with that language. Dosebai learnt with surprise that the bouquets thrown at the celebrated singer often contained bank notes, valuable rings and other precious things concealed within the fragrant flowers. She also noticed that the bouquets came mostly from the boxes occupied by the nobility. In her opinion, the people of England cared only for the higher sort of music and spent large sums of money on it. Not only the wealthy, but the middle classes were patrons too. The next day she paid visits to Mr and Mrs Wesche and Mr. Showell, ex-magistrate of Bombay. Both these families followed a much simpler lifestyle here in England compared to their mode of living in Bombay.

On 22nd July she received the sad tidings of the death of her uncle Sir Cowasjee Jehangir Readymoney, in Bombay.

Mr Gladstone was to speak in the House of Commons against the infamous Press Act, which had been framed by Lord Lytton's government. Mr. Fitzgerald, having very kindly sent Dosebai cards of admittance, off she went to the House of Commons. Mrs Gladstone, who was in the audience, enquired whether her husband's expected speech had drawn Dosebai there that day. Dosebai replied that as the topic was one relating to India, she was naturally very anxious to hear it discussed by statesmen like Mr. Gladstone. The scene was entirely unfamiliar to her, being the first political meeting she had ever attended. Here, she had the satisfaction of making the acquaintance of Mr. Fawcett, the blind philanthropist of India, and his wife. Who would not be touched at seeing this great man devoid of sight? He wore green spectacles on his sightless eyes and a young boy at his side guided his footsteps. He shook hands with Dosebai and enquired if she had obtained a good place at the House.

On returning from refreshments to the gallery, a lady came up to her and took out a slip of paper on which Dosebai's name was written in full and spelt correctly, but Dosebai had no idea who she was. She enquired of an official the name of the lady who had got her name so correctly, and was told that it was Mrs. Cavendish Bentinck. (The name suggests that she was connected to the family of the Dukes of Portland).

The members who took part in the discussions spoke very impressively and were listened to with the gravest attention. After Mr. Gladstone and some other members had spoken Professor Fawcett stood up and though deprived of sight, made a speech lasting over an hour and a half. The sight of this blind champion of India's rights and liberties as he stood there, giving utterance to his hopes and ambitions, was most inspiring to Dosebai, one of India's daughters. She was leaving her seat at 3 p.m. when Mrs Gladstone graciously shook hands with her and wished her well.

On the following day Dosebai paid a visit to Mr. Fawcett and in the evening, dined at Mr. Wesche's, and having an excess of energy, the day after that, she started for Brighton to see the Aquarium there. The climate of Brighton was more temperate than that of London. Having heard that Sir Albert Sassoon had a house at this place she went there to see if she could meet some member of the family, but to her regret, she found that Sir Albert had gone to Paris and his daughter Mrs. Gubbay, had left for Vienna. She discovered that their splendid residence was as grand as Buckingham Palace. The Sassoon family were the richest and most generous families to live in

Brighton and being on very friendly terms with the Prince of Wales (who became Edward VII), often accommodated the Prince on his several visits to King's Gardens, Brighton and Hove. After seeing the Aquarium, she took a train from Addison Road Station to Richmond, in Surrey, where the mother and children of her kind friend, Colonel Baker R.E., were living. Before she had left Bombay, Col. Baker had given her a letter of introduction to his mother, who had written to Dosebai, requesting her to come and see her at Richmond, as she was unable to travel to London.

The same evening, after returning home, she drove to Mrs. Cavendish Bentinck's, in Grafton Street and found her house to be a splendid mansion. Mrs. Bentinck enquired if Dosebai had been fortunate enough to meet Her Most Gracious Majesty the Queen Empress, and on her replying in the negative, she most kindly offered to present her if she would, after visiting Paris, come to Balmoral in Scotland, where Her Majesty would be in October. But to this kind proposal Dosebai could not accede, on account of the severity of the weather in Scotland. Nevertheless, she certainly thought about it!

Having, through the kindness of Mr. Fitzgerald, got a card of admission to see Windsor Castle, Dosebai and her son set off with great excitement. A guide was waiting to show them over and he gave them an in-depth history of the various kings and queens who had lived and died in this magnificent castle. The castle had a grand situation on a slight eminence and was surrounded by the beautiful and substantial Windsor Park. This commanding palace had a far nobler appearance than that of Buckingham Palace. The apartments occupied by the Royal family were, of course, very handsomely furnished. These private apartments were not usually open to visitors, but her special card of admission allowed her this privilege. Adjoining the castle stood the small but charmingly built Royal Chapel. Here she saw a fine marble group representing a beautiful woman with four sweet children clinging to her. This group, she later learnt, was meant to represent Virgin Mary and the four deceased children of the Royal family, one of these being the little son of the Princess Alice of Hesse, who had the misfortune to fall to his death from a window. She next visited the stables and left the castle at 5 p.m. Just as she was leaving, she saw Prince Leopold, the youngest of the Queen's sons, driving with his companions. Afterwards, she visited Virginia Water, a picturesque lake and the Deer Park.

On the 31st she had an invitation to see Mrs. Cavendish Bentinck again, and on her return, received a visit from Miss Manning. She also paid another visit on the 4th of August, to Mrs. Baker at Richmond. On her way home she wandered around Kew Gardens. When one considers that travel was only by carriage and horse, the energy of this woman seems absolutely astounding. Reaching home at 7 o'clock, she found a note from her valued friend, Mrs Cavendish Bentinck, enclosing a ticket for a box at the theatre. She felt herself to be under the greatest obligation to her and in her autobiography, took the opportunity of again expressing her grateful sentiments for many a favour shown to her during her first voyage to England.

CHAPTER 18

AT THE PARIS EXHIBITION

On the 9th of August 1878, after breakfast at seven o'clock, Dosebai and her son bade adieu to the place where they had put up for the last six weeks. Starting from Charing Cross Station they reached Dover Pier at 9.30 and going on board the twin-deck mail steamer, left the shores of England. The English Channel was said to be very rough, but they found it calm; the atmosphere was sultry but the passage of about two hours duration was very smooth and enjoyable. Amongst the passengers was a genial lady named Mrs. Lyons, with whom she had a long chat. This lady knew several of the Parsi residents of Paris, of whom she gave a very good report. One of these, Mr Perojshaw Ruttonjee Cama, had left his family, and was leading the life of a recluse in Europe. Previous to Dosebai's departure from Bombay, his mother had earnestly requested her to find her son's whereabouts and to write to her full particulars about him and this, Dosebai hoped to be able to do. At noon they landed at Calais and immediately took the train for Paris, which they reached in the evening. The station – the *Gare du Nord* – was so excessively crowded that she would have found it extremely difficult to get out of it at all, had not Mr. Lyons kindly assisted them in getting their luggage examined and escorting them to a cab.

This gentleman recommended them to go to the Hotel Mirabeau, where he assured them they would be comfortable and where they would find several Parsi gentlemen lodged. (Bear in mind that their womenfolk did not travel afar in those days). They accordingly drove thither, and after supper there came several Parsi gentlemen of her acquaintance to see her. During their conversation, when she enquired after the elusive Mr. Cama, they told her that it would be next to impossible to see young Perojshaw for, were he to hear that anyone from Bombay had been enquiring after him, he would at once change his quarters and disappear, but undaunted, she resolved to try and see him early the next morning. Accordingly after breakfast, she set out in quest of Mr. Cama but found to her regret and surprise, that he had already left his lodgings the night before and vanished, nobody knew where.

Provided with a note from Mrs. Cavendish Bentinck, Dosebai next went to find some lodgings, which that lady had recommended to her. It was past 2 o'clock ere she succeeded in reaching her destination. The landlady was pleased on reading Mrs. Bentinck's note, but showed her disappointment at being unable to accommodate them as all her rooms were occupied. She recommended the new Continental Hotel to Dosebai, so she instructed the coachman to drive them there. On the way, she met one of her countrymen, Mr. Jamsetjee Dastoor, who kindly accompanied them to the hotel. She engaged a couple of rooms on the third floor at a cost of Rs.15 a day, which was reasonable enough. These rooms were, of course, smaller in size than some others whose rent was exorbitant, but they were equally well provided with the necessities and comforts of life. Indeed, what she had been allowed to view and admire at a distance in London was in reality all around here. On the day of her arrival, she went and sat down in the drawing room and no sooner had she done so, than the other occupants of the room became interested in her. Some began to walk around her and scan her dress, and some addressed her but as she could not understand French, conversation was impossible between them, till an American girl asked her if she knew English and upon answering in the affirmative, she very gladly became the interpreter.

While they were chatting, the dinner bell rang. Dosebai and her son took the seats that had been reserved for them at a table capable of accommodating a hundred and fifty to two hundred persons or even more. She found the French dishes very much to her liking, for they closely resembled Parsi cuisine. This was probably due to the abundant use of onions, garlic and herbs in French cooking. After a sumptuous repast they adjourned to the drawing room and entered into conversation with the ladies assembled there, with whom she soon became familiar.

On the morning of the 11th on descending to the dining room, she found groups of people seated round small tables taking breakfast. She ordered her simple meal of bread and coffee; both of which she found excellent. (Good choice, in France)! Mr. Jamsetjee came to escort them to the Exhibition, and on seeing him, her heart was set at rest for he could speak French as fluently as a Parisian. After an hour's drive they reached the Exhibition, the great dome of which they had seen from afar. The dimensions of the Trocadero Palace were massive, using the latest technology of the time to prove that French architecture and builders could outdo the English. The size of the main auditorium surpassed that of its English competitor, the Albert Hall. The dome of the Trocadero was almost twenty-three feet higher than the dome of St. Peters, and the towers were taller than those of Notre Dame by forty-five feet. This was perhaps the beginning of a movement that would culminate eleven years later with the building of the Eiffel Tower.

Even at that early hour, there were no fewer than ten thousand people assembled there. Dosebai was a bit scared of mingling in such an intense crowd. However, she took her ticket and entered the garden, from which one could go to the various amusements at the Exhibition. Having, with her companion and son, entered the Exhibition grounds she found herself speedily surrounded by a mass of people interested in her Parsi attire. However, thanks to the tact of Mr. Jamsetjee, who replied in different languages to all who were curious enough to question him about her, she felt no inconvenience or difficulty. The police were on the alert too, and as (*comme l'habitude*), she had on her person all the jewellery and ornaments customary amongst the Parsis, the well meaning out of the crowd advised her to be very careful. With great courtesy the people made way for her, and she decided that politeness was a typical French characteristic. Dear reader, you are permitted a little smile.

Crossing the Pont d'Iena from the Trocadero Park, the visitor saw the impressive façade, constructed by Gustave Eiffel, of the main exhibition building. The iron beams of the Palace of Industry were painted blue and all along the lower storey of the entranceway and facing the Seine were twenty-two 'Statues of the Powers', sculptures representing the major nations taking part in the Exhibition. India was represented as 'British India' and there was no statue representing Germany as France was not yet willing to forgive or forget the Franco-Prussian War (1870 -71).

The area of the ground of the Great Exhibition was equal to that of a good sized town, and it was divided into about thirty distinct courts, as each country of the world was represented by a court specially set apart for it. It was a 'Street of Nations', each one entered by a splendid life sized gateway representing the country. Besides the countless articles exhibited there, such as jewellery, piece goods, metal work, articles of stone, wood and china, there was machinery at work, demonstrating how all these things were made from raw materials. They saw how diamonds were polished, how steel pens, pins and needles were made, how porcelain, crockery and glass was moulded, how furnishing fabrics were produced and, most interesting of all, how fine lace was made. There was instantaneous photography, painting at sight, machine-made jewellery, imitation jewellery in glass, stone and metals, and some pieces worked intricately in filigree. Pretty young girls were to be seen blowing glass into a thousand and one knick-knacks with astonishing skill. The wide-eyed Dosebai decided that it was infinitely better to incur fatigue and danger and see the wonders of the world, than to live a long life of idleness and luxury.

When she was in London, she had wanted to visit Liverpool, Birmingham, Manchester and other well known centres of industry, but her friends dissuaded her from doing so and advised her to see the Great Exhibition instead, saying it was a compendium of all the curious, notable and elegant productions and sights of the world that the age could produce. This she found fully verified and was therefore very grateful to her kind advisers. Led on by an eager impulse to see everything, she never faltered till 2 o'clock, when she began to flag, so they went and had some lunch in one of the many restaurants at the exhibition. As this was the usual hour for that meal, the crowd of hungry visitors was enormous and the hurry and bustle brought to her mind a public dinner in Bombay. They turned again to see the Exhibition, for they had seen till then but an infinitesimal part of it. Wherever she looked, she saw such novelties that had her means permitted, she would have made many purchases. During her stay in London she had not seen anything that would bear comparison with what she saw in Paris in so short a time; in fact this marvellous Exhibition had culled the choicest products of more than thirty countries, and they thanked God for having allowed them the privilege of seeing it. Her utmost ambition had been to visit England, but God had not only granted that ambition of hers, but had also graciously crowned her utmost hopes by bringing her to see this stupendous Exhibition teeming with thousands of wonders.

On the morrow, they visited the Exhibition again. The fee for admission was only one franc and yet what a large amount must have been realised by the daily receipts, the average number of visitors being 50,000 per day since the opening of the exhibition three months before. This fact alone was proof of the universal interest and attraction of the Exhibition. With true feminine curiosity, her mind was set upon seeing the jewellery, and she saw, amongst other articles, a pair of large pearls – the size of sparrow eggs – which in her opinion, was the best of the whole collection. Much pleased with what they saw, they left the Exhibition in the evening and crossed the river in a steam launch from which they enjoyed the views of this beautiful city.

On the following day, Dosebai went to make arrangements for the despatch of their luggage and to secure passage from Brindisi to Bombay and also visited the Exhibition once more. Returning to the hotel in the evening, she had a chat with the other visitors, amongst whom were the American Consul, Mr. B. J. Beiscotto and a Mr. and Mrs. Kirby who like herself, had left their native country to come and see the exhibition. They intended to stay a considerable time in Paris and wished her to do likewise and then go with them to America. She found the American people frank, polite and independent and what is still better, without pride, so that the rich and the poor associated together without any reserve.

CHAPTER 19

DOSEBAI'S ASCENT IN A BALLOON

The next morning, the intrepid Dosebai heard that a hot air balloon was to ascend from the Trocadero and that anyone who wanted to could enjoy the novel pleasure of an aerial sail. Her friends at the hotel were surprised to hear that she ardently longed to go up in the balloon and asked her whether all Parsi women were of a bold, adventurous nature like herself. She had to dispel this very erroneous idea by telling them that a few years ago, Parsi women and even a few of the men, were so frightened of Europeans that they would run away if they saw any approaching them. She however, by her early associations with Europeans had acquired their tastes and some of their courage. These remarks pleased her American friends, who again urged her to visit New York, most hospitably extracting from her a promise that when she did so, she should go to no hotel or boarding house but stay with them.

Dressing herself in warm clothing and carrying in a handbag some notepaper, a flask of brandy, biscuits and a piece of iron to which to attach any missive she might wish to send down to people below (what was she thinking of), she set out for the place from which the ascent was to take place. Here, there was an enormous crowd whose amazement at seeing her amongst the aeronauts was most amusing to behold. On payment of a sum of Rs.10 Dosebai took her seat. This balloon, being intended merely for pleasure excursions, was attached to the earth by a very long rope. There were in all, fifteen passengers, three of whom were ladies. She did not allow Dadabhoy to accompany her for fear of an accident.

At 5 p.m. they began to ascend slowly and she saw the earth receding from beneath them. Presently, the panorama that spread itself out before them as they hovered over the splendid city was most strange and fantastic; the people they had left below might have been taken for a swarm of bees, the river Seine with its stately bridges, the gardens with their flowers and ancient trees, the fountains with their feeble jets of water vainly trying to reach the sky, the proud monuments, the magnificent buildings and their tall spires, the majestic Opera House, the thousands of boats darting like fishes hither and thither on the water, the Exhibition, from which hundreds of flags were gaily waving, and the innumerable other places of interest in this wonderful city, formed a scene which looked like something out of fairyland, in her own words, 'it seemed a faint reflex of the unfading lustre and undying joy of Paradise itself!'

How long she wondered, would her wealthy sisters shut themselves up in their old habits and prejudices, shunning healthy and ennobling pleasures, which lay alluringly at their very door! Why did they cling so tenaciously to their idle crude customs and know no higher ambition than to glide along in the same groove as their ancestors, instead of proving themselves worthy of the times they lived in by basking in the free air of enlightenment! Her own thoughts, while looking down at the Earth, 'Awake, dear sisters, ere the stealthy hand of Time rob you of youth and opportunity to learn wisdom! To die in the hope of entering Paradise is blessed, but thrice blessed is he who, living a life of piety and virtue, learns something of the world he lives in and of the other races of mankind who share it with him.'

But to return to the point – as the balloon rose higher and higher, the cold became more intense, and she began to shiver. She had to take a good draught of the brandy she had prudently brought with her. She offered some to a lady who looked rather frail and who was most grateful for the offer. They had now risen to the full height allowed by the rope, namely, 700 metres, and she experienced an exhilarating sensation of pleasure in soaring like a bird above the Earth – a pleasure enhanced by the knowledge that they were safely tethered to Mother earth and that all precautions were being taken to preserve the balloon in the upright position. As they began to descend, Paris, which had dwindled into an insignificant speck, gradually assumed her own graceful dimensions and they were soon deposited on terra firma, after an aerial flight of forty-five minutes. A medal commemorating the ascent was presented to each passenger. Oh! For words to describe this exciting adventure!

As the gardens of the Tuileries had attracted her notice from the balloon, they then went there, and found much to admire. It covered a large area and was rich in flowers, lawns, avenues, trees, statues and fountains. An old fashioned and stately atmosphere pervaded the place. The palace had been in a state of dilapidation since the Franco-German war, but was imposing in its very ruins.

On 16th August, after writing letters to Bombay, London and Germany, they returned to the Exhibition and spent the whole day in looking at the fine collection of paintings but it would have needed a full month to see them all thoroughly, so immense was the number. Some of the pictures were valued at from a lakh (Rs. 100,000) and a lakh and a half of rupees – almost incredible to the Indian mind. On the 17th she went to a jeweller's and ordered some ornaments to be sent out to her in India and on returning, heard from her son of his having, quite by chance, met a gentleman of the firm of Messrs. Fallek, after they had given up all hopes of seeing anyone from that firm. Messrs. Fallek, while in Bombay ten years before, were in the habit of coming to their place to negotiate, through her husband, for the purchase of pearls. This gentleman was very pleased at their being in Paris and invited them to spend the evening at his house. Then they went to a studio and had themselves photographed.

On the 18th, after breakfast, she started by train for Versailles, which was reached in half an hour. This was a national fete day, an anniversary on which the fountains played and crowds of people flocked to see them. Within an enclosure, the beautifully designed garden lay in its smiling beauty, interspersed with alabaster equestrian statues. Proceeding along the avenue, they came in sight of the celebrated Palace of Versailles – a building worthy of such opulent surroundings. As she entered the spacious hall, an Englishman named Mr Cuthbert, politely enquired if she had been there before and as it was difficult to see all the places of interest in the palace without guidance, he most kindly offered assistance and she most gladly availed herself of it. The palace was divided into many suites of apartments, each in the charge of an official, who conducted the visitors through the suite and gave an account of everything contained therein. Mr Cuthbert kindly translated for her as they went along. The ancient furniture was so beautifully polished that it looked quite new. There were splendid old paintings in all the rooms and entire walls of several others were hung with tapestry representing battle scenes. The spectacular Hall of Mirrors took their breath away and the palace contained so many interesting objects, that they were worn out just looking at them. The ceiling of the dining hall was exquisitely painted with figures of fairies in gold and silver and it was almost too much to take in.

In the grounds, there were four other equally splendid palaces standing at a mile distance from each other in the garden. The extent of the garden could be judged by this fact but its beauty had to be seen to be believed. The garden was designed in the 17th Century, by André le Notre and was a terrestrial Eden. There were a number of cool retreats and shady arbours. Undulating expanses of ground were covered over with luxuriant grass, romantic lakes lay at the foot of hills and swiftly flowing streams meandered through the lovely landscape. In short, nature and art had combined to create a masterpiece. They saw a number of carriages, which had belonged to Louis XIV and Napoleon Bonaparte. They were richly gilded and painted with birds and the seats were covered with velvet and adorned with gold and silver tassels.

Proceeding further, Mr. Cuthbert exclaimed: 'Here is the centre of attraction!' And so it was, truly. They stood before an enormous pool of water in which about a hundred powerful fountains were playing among the most fantastic statues. Some represented a tree with its trunk, branches, twigs and leaves, others assumed a thousand fanciful shapes as they rose and fell, while the largest and most impressive, which only played once a year on this day, represented mighty Neptune, the God of Water. In this one figure, there must have been at least a thousand jets at play; the air around was thereby rendered as moist as in the rainy season. There were seats arranged as in a theatre down to the very margin of the lake for the convenience of the numerous spectators. Dosebai was totally bowled over with the marvellous beauty of this enchanting scene.

After breakfast on the 22nd of August, she went, with Mr. and Mrs. Kirby and their daughters to Bon Marché, one of the most fashionable shops in Paris, in size and magnificence a veritable palace. It was difficult in the midst of so many beautiful things in the emporium to make a choice, but at last she selected some silks, fans, handkerchiefs and woollen fabrics. One of the superintendents kindly showed her over the entire establishment, saying that their shop was never before graced by the presence of a lady of her race and dress and the entire staff had therefore stopped work to look at her. Highly delighted, she visited this shop again on the 23rd and 24th to make some more purchases. (That was, surely, the secret of their success).

Two days were spent in leave-taking and making preparations for their departure, and on the 28th she went and bought Cook's Tickets for herself and her son and then went to have a last look at the Exhibition. Returning again after dinner to the Trocadero, they took a sorrowful farewell of this unparalleled Exhibition, which had been the main incentive for her crossing the ocean. The last evening at the hotel was spent in the company of friends so they pledged each other's health and spoke of meeting again. She received visits from Messrs. Fallek and other friends, as also letters from her friends in Germany, who were excitedly awaiting her intended visit to them. Glad as she was on the one hand, she was sorely aggrieved on the other at hearing from Bombay that her dear husband was having some business problems. Although this news occasioned her great chagrin she did not give way to despair, but confined her travels on the Continent to Germany, Italy and Switzerland only, and relinquished the half-formed plan of returning to London and seeing Scotland, Balmoral and above all, Queen Victoria.

On the 29th she was engaged all morning in packing her luggage and settling accounts with the jewellers and the hotel, and giving gratuities to the attendants. The general manager of the hotel, who had obliged them in a variety of ways, only asked for her photograph, which she willingly gave him. Parting is always attended with pain. This she felt when bidding a temporary farewell to her native place, Bombay. The great regret that her husband whose kind indulgence procured her all these enjoyments did not share them with her, was never for a moment absent from her mind, but she never ceased to entertain the hope that God Almighty would one day permit them to revisit Europe together, which hope alas, was never realised.

From the Hotel they went to the *Gare du Nord* and boarded the train for Cologne.

CHAPTER 20

MEETING MRS. AHLERS AT BONN

They reached the station of Cologne at daybreak on the 30th of
August where her closest friend, towards whom she felt the affection
and confidence of a sister, was awaiting their arrival. This lady was
Mrs. Ahlers, widow of Rudolph Ahlers chief partner of Messrs.
Volkart Bros. The closest friendship had long existed between
Dosebai's family and this amiable pair.

Mr. and Mrs. Ahlers left Bombay in 1869 and were leading a very
happy life in London, till the untimely death of Mr. Ahlers in 1876
plunged his poor wife, his children and his numerous friends into
profound grief. Ten long years had passed since they had seen each
other. At the station, Mrs Ahlers ran up and embraced her, but grief
had wrought such a dire change in her that Dosebai would never
have known her again. She was dressed in black and a deep shade of
melancholy had settled on her once joyful face. 'Since I lost my
husband three years ago,' she said, with a heavy sigh, ' the world has
been a blank wilderness to me, but now I have some cause to rejoice
in meeting my old friend'. After breakfast, which Mrs. Ahlers had
got ready for them at the station, they entered the train together and
reached Bonn at 11 am. Dosebai expressed her dearest wish to see
Mrs. Ahler's children, but they were to arrive the next day.

A friend and neighbour of Mrs. Ahlers, a Professor and a man
advanced in years as well as in learning, came to see them and invite
them to lunch. His wife and children were spending the vacation in
England. He was a very jolly German and though he could only
converse through Mrs. Ahlers as interpreter, they soon became
friends. Returning from the Professor's house at three o'clock, she
took a little rest, after which her friend took her for a drive to see the
town. Bonn, situated on the beautiful river Rhine, was a pretty town
with its villas surrounded by lovely gardens and many trees. The

view of the Seven Mountains all around combined to give it a cool and pleasant appearance. It was the seat of a celebrated university to which students came from all parts of the world and the climate was wonderful. Also, living here was cheaper than in England, for which reason her friend had chosen it for the education of her young children.

On coming down to breakfast the next morning she found, to her great joy, that the children had arrived. They had been given to understand that their mother's brother and sister had come to see them, and in this expectation they came bounding up but stopped abruptly on seeing her strange dress. Their mother reassured them and they then embraced Dosebai, so that she felt as much satisfied as if their lamented father, their esteemed friend, stood before them. Very soon these sweet children, a boy and two little girls, had become so familiar with Dosebai that they could scarcely separate when bedtime came.

The whole of the next day was spent in the children's company and in the evening they dined at the Professor's, where Dosebai made the acquaintance of the Misses Allan-Olney, who were much interested in her nationality. The next day these ladies called and received her photograph. At the happy suggestion of her dearest friend, she and her children, Dosebai and her son went and had themselves photographed in a group, as a souvenir of her visit. She had with her a set of Delhi ornaments, which Mrs. Ahlers accepted and wore on this occasion. This day was the anniversary of the battle of Sédan, which took place on 1st September 1870 (part of the Franco-Prussian war and a decisive German victory, which led to the fall of the second French Empire and capture of Napoleon III). The town was gaily decorated for the holiday.

The same evening, she went with her friend to a small party. On the 4th they had a delightful excursion to the Drachenfels (or Dragonrock), one of the Seven Mountains about half an hour's journey from Bonn, and on the 5th, after breakfast, she went to have another photograph taken. The photographer here, like his brethren of London and Paris, begged to be allowed to take a life-sized portrait for himself, the singularity of her dress making her an interesting subject to him and his fraternity.

The next day they were ready for departure. As the time for parting drew nigh, they grew very sad. She was loath to leave the congenial company of her friend and her children, but she drew consolation from the resolve that, if God were to spare her life, she would return. On the morning of the 7th of September, they all sat down together for the last time to an early breakfast, the children pressing round her crying, 'Aunty, don't go to your own country and leave us'. She felt parting from them as keenly as if she were tearing herself away from her own family. They went to the station accompanied by the good old Professor, whom she warmly thanked for his kindness and hospitality. Taking a tender farewell of Mrs. Ahlers and her children, she and her son entered the train and were carried away from the good town of Bonn, the little friendly group standing on the platform waving caps and handkerchiefs till they were out of sight.

They made a brief stopover in Mayence, where they were met by a servant of Monsieur Knoop's and a couple of landaus that had been sent to convey them and their luggage to that gentleman's house at Wiesbaden, about an hour's distance. The roads and two-storeyed houses here bore a strong resemblance to those of Bombay, and the drive reminded her of her trip from Tardeo to Bhandoop. The carriage drew up under the portico of a grand mansion, very similar to Sir Albert Sassoon's 'Sans Souci' in Bombay. She was warmly welcomed by Mr & Mme. Knoop and after a few kind enquiries about Dosebai's health and the journey, Mme. Knoop took her upstairs to select for herself whatever suite of rooms she preferred but Dosebai informed her that her stay would only be of a few hours' duration. She had seen enough of the grandeur of Europe and it was only for the purpose of making their acquaintance and of conversing on some business matters that she had intruded upon their hospitality.

When lunch was announced, Monsieur Knoop led Dosebai in on his arm and she had the pleasure of seeing at the table, Mr. Muller, a partner of Messrs. Knoop and Co., who had, in company with Mr Ahlers, often visited her at her house in Bombay. After an interval of twelve years they met here quite unexpectedly, and they mutually expressed joy at seeing each other again. Mr. Muller said, ' You have not changed in the least, except that you have not got the large nose-ring pendant from your nose which I used to see before'. He had been a guest at Dosebai's children's weddings, where he had observed her wear this ornament, then in general use amongst Parsi women but now brought into disuse by time and fashion. After lunch, Madame Knoop gave her a tour of the whole house, furnished with regal splendour. Monsieur Knoop was an influential and highly respected citizen of Wiesbaden and it was said that the Emperor William once honoured this palatial residence with his presence.

The long drive back to Mayence was most enjoyable, the beautiful verdant landscape being illuminated by a flood of silver moonlight. Leaving Mayence at 10 pm they reached Bahl (Basel) at daybreak.

Taking the morning train, they reached Constance at 3 pm, where she found her old friend, first known as Mrs. George Volkart, now Mme Amman, with her stepson, waiting for her at the station. Eighteen years had elapsed since they had last met but she had the same healthy and bonny appearance as always and Dosebai was delighted at seeing her again and in such good circumstances. They drove to her villa on the lake. Lake Constance was in extent like a sea and totally stunning with greenery all round backed by the snow-capped mountains. Mme Amman and Dosebai had much to say to each other of all that had happened to them since they had last met. Dosebai informed her friend that she could be her guest for only one day.

In the evening they sat on the balcony enjoying the scenery, the villa being built on the very margin of the lake. As this was a national holiday, the lake was full of pleasure boats and delicious strains of music wafted to their ears over the glassy surface of the waters. Her good friend had prepared special accommodation for Dosebai's comfort and when she rose the next morning and looked out, the house appeared as it were, to be standing in the middle of a sea. The scene was completely different to the evening before and even more beautiful. After breakfast she told Mme. Amman all about her travels in India and Europe. Mrs Amman listened to them with unfeigned surprise, for she had remained sufficiently long in Bombay to know the timidity of the Parsis and their retiring disposition and though she had often met Dosebai in English society, she had no idea of her sense of adventure.

They then went into the town of Constance to see Mme. Amman's winter residence, which was a spacious and elegantly furnished house with all the comforts and luxuries Dosebai had seen at the Knoop residence. Returning to the villa, they sat down to dinner, after which young Mr. Amman took his leave as he was going to Winterthur to join his father. He begged Dosebai and Dadabhoy to accompany him, assuring them that the Volkart family at Winterthur would bitterly regret not seeing them. But as their time was limited and she had a longing to see Rome, she had to decline the offer. That afternoon, they started on a return journey to Bahl – both in going and returning they had a glimpse from the train of the spectacular Falls of the Rhine at Schaffhausen. The scenery of Lake Constance and the River Rhine was romantic in the extreme. She was particularly struck with the abundance and luxuriant growth of the Araucaria (a variety of evergreen conifer) trees. They reached Bahl again at 9 pm and crossing a beautiful bridge over the Rhine, arrived at the Hotel Schweizerhof, where they were given pleasant rooms on the first floor.

They took the morning train for Geneva. The entire journey was through superbly sublime Swiss mountain scenery. The vertiginous railway track, perched on the mountain edge and winding in a serpentine course over it, was perilously exciting. They reached Geneva, the most beautiful city in Switzerland, the land of beauty, that afternoon and after depositing their luggage at Pension Windsor, hired a carriage for a drive through the city. After a short but very sweet stay, they left Geneva the same evening.

The joy of travelling first class was that you generally had the whole compartment to yourself. On this occasion, however, a male passenger entered their carriage and he was so intoxicated that they feared a disturbance for, notwithstanding the remonstrance of Dadabhoy, he insisted on sitting close to them. At the next station they complained, and the stationmaster had him removed. (Now, that's what you call service). They reached Modane early the next morning having passed through the Mont Cenis Tunnel, which was then the longest tunnel in the world (built in 1871, it was eight and a half miles long) and took half an hour to traverse. They saw thousands of workmen working here illuminated by flaming torches. Taking another train from Bardonecchia, they reached Turin at nine o'clock, where they stopped for an hour for breakfast. They passed in the course of the day, many cities of note and antiquity, such as Parma, Bologna (with the oldest Italian University), and Ravenna. The bird's eye glimpse from the train was enchanting and made her long to make another visit. At nine o'clock that evening, they arrived in Florence, 'The Beautiful'. The station was splendid and very busy. After an Italian supper in the refreshment room, which was as large and brilliantly lit as a palace or the best Parisian hotel, they resumed their journey to Rome. What a pity she did not stop over in Florence.

With Mrs. Ahlers and her children at Bonn

CHAPTER 21

ROME – AND A PRIVATE AUDIENCE WITH THE POPE

At daybreak, on 12th September 1878 they reached Rome, the capital of Italy, immortalised in the history of the ancient world. The station was very crowded and of course, everyone spoke Italian and they did not. However, people were extremely helpful and when Dosebai showed her card of recommendation for the Anglo-American Hotel, they were taken there. Welcomed by the manager, they were offered a comfortable, well-furnished apartment on the first floor. After a refreshing bath and a good breakfast they set off to view the city with an English-speaking guide.

Dosebai gazed with awe and admiration at the architectural glories of a former age, now crumbling to decay, but magnificent even in their ruins. Their guide took them from one celebrated place to another, giving them an outline of the history of each one. They saw the walls and gates of Rome, the Arch of Titus, the Arch of Constantine, the Pantheon, the Basilica of St. Lateran, the Museum, the Colosseum, the Temple of Venus, the Sancta Scala, St. Pietro Vinculi, the Column of Constantine, the Palace of the Caesars, Trajan's Column and many statues, arches and fountains. The gardens were, in many instances, now wildernesses overgrown with weeds. (The natural wildflower meadow look was not yet fashionable, then).

Proceeding beyond the fort, they approached the Church of St. Paul, which from outside presented no special feature except that of its height and solitary position. On alighting from her carriage, she noticed a great many poor people about the doors asking for alms. Entering the noble doorway, what a splendid sight burst upon their gaze! The whole of the grand hall was paved with highly polished

142

blocks of marble, each of them larger than she had seen elsewhere. These huge slabs of marble were arranged so as to represent the white billows of the ocean. Lifting their eyes to the ceiling, they were again lost in admiration, for there the limner's art had produced a masterpiece, representing a crown supported by aerial creatures of wondrous beauty and grace. High up in niches in the wall, stood life-sized marble statues of various Popes over the centuries, giving evidence of the perfection to which the art of sculpture was brought so many years ago.

Dosebai had seen many spectacular buildings before, but none, in her opinion, was at all comparable to this magnificent church – all others paled before it, as the moon before the sun, and it was no exaggeration to say that that if anything could illustrate the exalted beauty of Paradise, it must surely be this wonderful place. In her estimation, this edifice was the ultimate in architectural perfection.

They also visited the ruins of a mighty amphitheatre built by the Romans, about 2,500 years ago and known as the theatre of Marcellus. After seeing other interesting memorials of past ages they threaded their way back to the hotel through narrow streets. After an hour's rest, they started again with their guide.

This time, they headed for St. Peter's Basilica, (Basilica Sancti Petri), an Italian Renaissance church in Vatican City, the papal enclave within the city of Rome. Designed mainly by Donato Bramante, Michelangelo, Carlo Maderno and Gian Lorenzo Bernini, St. Peter's was the most renowned work of Renaissance architecture and also, the largest church in the world. St. Peter's was regarded as the holiest of Catholic shrines.

Catholic tradition holds that the Basilica was the burial site of St. Peter, one of Jesus's Apostles and also the first Pope. Saint Peter's tomb was, supposedly, directly below the high altar of the Basilica.

Next, they went to see the Vatican, the Palace of the Pope, which adjoins the Basilica. The picture gallery was the most celebrated in the world, as it contained the masterpieces of the ancient Roman painters, the models from which artists of all future ages had studied their art. While walking here, they were met by Cardinal Macchi who entered into conversation, asking about their parentage, caste and religion, showing great interest in the fact that they were Zoroastrians. Dosebai expressed her great wish to see His Holiness the Pope, whereupon the Cardinal replied that the Holy Father could be seen every fortnight when presiding at a congregation but as the last one had taken place only the day before, it would be thirteen days before the next opportunity of seeing him would occur.

'My stay here', she said, 'will not be more than two days as I have come merely to see this celebrated city and the finest churches in the world.' The Cardinal seemed very pleased at this and asked if she really was very anxious to see the Holy Father, to which she replied, of course, in the affirmative. They then parted and continued on their way to the summit of the hill, Janiculum, which commanded a panoramic view of the city and the surrounding country. From there, they strolled through the extensive Borghese Gardens, then along the banks of the Tiber and through the public thoroughfares, reaching their hotel at 7 p.m.

A note was waiting for Dosebai the next morning. Her guide read it as it was in Italian and expressed his great astonishment, for it was from Pope Leo XIII himself who, hearing from Cardinal Macchi of her great desire to see him, invited her to come at 4 o'clock that very afternoon, when he would grant her an interview and give her a blessing. Her friends at the hotel congratulated her on this unexpected honour, as it was known that His Holiness only accorded an audience to those who made a written application for it, which however was at the option of the Pope to grant or refuse. This gracious invitation threw her into a dilemma, as all her best outfits were packed up and sent to Brindisi and she was here with only plain clothes, suitable for travelling. To appear before a personage more eminent than even an Emperor in such everyday clothes would be rather rude, and so she asked her guide to go to Cardinal Macchi and ask whether it would not be deemed an insult to appear at the audience in such a dress as he had seen her in yesterday, but his reply dispelled all her fears. To feel suitably attired, she put on every bit of her priceless jewellery, as she carried them about with her wherever she went, and carefully concealed them under her sari, so that even the guide who went with them could not have guessed that she was wearing them, which was probably a very wise idea.

They drove to the Vatican and were conducted up a noble flight of stairs to the first landing, where two sentinels in full military uniform were stationed. Here, a priest who spoke English met her. He congratulated her on the distinguished honour conferred upon her by His Holiness and then began to explain the rules of etiquette to be observed at the interview. Dosebai, on hearing that she should have to kiss the Pope's toe, promptly expressed objection, for though right and fitting to pay due homage to one whom God has raised to such a high position, such an act as kissing one's toe would be considered most unhygienic. She said this to the priest and added, 'Very exact are the observances enjoined by my religion and I always hold them in high esteem'. Approving her explanation in justification of her objection, he led her through the Palace. Two soldiers guarded every room and landing and after passing through seven rooms they reached a magnificent hall, where she was asked to take a seat. This room and the furniture were all bright red – and the guards who patrolled here were dressed, even to their boots, in the same flaming hue. Presently, the priest returned, and requested her to kneel down on receiving the Pope's benediction and to kiss the fingers of his hand, which he would extend to her instead of his foot.

He then brought Dosebai to another hall, painted and furnished entirely in pure white; here she saw a revered person of angelic appearance coming towards them at a slow, measured pace. At the sight of this thrice-holy man, they knelt down. At that moment, she felt such ecstatic joy as could not be described – what, she supposed, one would experience in the presence of a prophet, or a being of another world. The Holy Father had the majesty and the aspect of an angel. He wore white robes, with a white cap upon his head. In a clear melodious voice, he poured his benediction upon Dosebai and her son, after which he condescended to converse with her. Their conversation was carried on with the Cardinal interpreting, and the following is the substance of it. After placing his blessed hand on her head, he said, 'May you live long and be firm in your faith whereby all your best aspirations will be fulfilled'. Taking out her watch and showing him the beautifully enamelled portraits of her dear husband and children on its lid, she asked him to bless them with long life.

With a broad smile on his kindly countenance, he blessed her in these words; - 'May God fulfil your best wishes and may you reap manifold advantages from your long and arduous travels when you shall have reached your own shores in peace and safety.'

'Pray, hand me your card', he said, ' that I may remember you in my prayers and invoke the assistance of God on your every laudable undertaking'. He continued 'You must surely have been much pleased with the beautiful churches of St. Peter and St. Paul, ' whereupon she respectfully informed him that she had seen both these celebrated buildings, of which the magnificence would live in her memory forever, and the few days spent in Rome would rank amongst the happiest of her life. The Pope then asked her to stay for a month, when his Cardinal would introduce her to the reigning Sovereign of Italy, King Victor Emmanuel. Gratifying as this gracious proposal was, she had to decline, as her stay in the Eternal City could not be prolonged. She further informed His Holiness that she had at first, only intended to stay for two days in that imperial city but having been favoured by an interview with such an exalted, estimable and worthy potentate as His Holiness, she had resolved to stay a few days longer, though all her luggage had been sent off to Brindisi. She then asked if His Holiness would be pleased to keep her photograph in his majestic Palace and he, with much pleasure, ordered his Cardinal to accept the picture, as the Pope never accepted anything, except through one of his Cardinals. Their conversation lasted about an hour and they then took their leave, enriched by his many benedictions.

On the 14th after tiffin (old British word for lunch), they went to see the King's Palace. As King Victor Emmanuel was away on tour through his dominions, they were permitted to enter without much ado.

They left Rome that evening, arriving at Cazerta the next morning. This was an hour's journey from Naples, but to see this city, second only to Rome, she should have had to cancel her through ticket to Brindisi. This, she did not feel inclined to do and therefore continued her journey through the fruit growing districts of Italy and reached Brindisi the following morning. Here, she found young Mr. Amman waiting for her, as he was also going to India by the mail.

Dosebai's tour in Europe was now brought to a close and she longed to see her family in Bombay, but she was grieved to part from her son Dadabhoy, who had been her constant companion on her travels, and who was now going back to London to complete his professional studies.

She embarked on board the P&O Steamer 'Ceylon' and passed the first two days in melancholy loneliness, but after that, she began to mix with her fellow-passengers, who were very agreeable and cheerful. On the fourth day they reached Alexandria early in the morning and she went ashore with Mr. Amman and two other young gentlemen. The town bore a grand, evocative name reminding one of the great Conqueror who in ages gone by, governed the whole known world, but squalor and dirt prevailed here and Dosebai was not impressed. In the evening they started by train from the Alexandria Railway Station, and reached Suez the next morning where the steamship 'Geelong' was waiting for them.

The weather in the Red Sea was extremely hot and sticky, in consequence of which, most of the passengers slept on deck. She would not do so and was nearly roasted alive in her cabin. However, the company on board was refined and agreeable and as some of the passengers were good vocalists the time passed smoothly along. A lottery was started, to which each subscriber contributed Rs 5. About Rs. 125 were collected and much to her delight, this sum fell to her lot. They reached Aden on 25th September, but this time she did not go on shore.

On the 3rd October the S.S. Geelong anchored in Bombay harbour. Her husband, whom she had appraised of her arrival by telegram from Aden, had been most uneasy at the delay caused by an accident on their way from Aden to Bombay and now he, with her second son, came on board and heartfelt was their joy at meeting again and finding each other safe and well. Shaking hands with the Captain and all her fellow passengers, she bade 'adieu' to the *'S.S. Geelong'*.

CHAPTER 22

THE UPS AND DOWNS OF LIFE

While in Paris, Dosebai had heard much from the friendly and hospitable Americans at the hotel about the grandeur of their country so she resolved to convince her husband to go on a world voyage with her. She suggested finding a tenant for their bungalow, and discovered that Mr. Vincent, the Deputy Commissioner of Police, wished to take it up on a long lease. He even consented to their retaining possession of a small bungalow within the compound into which they accordingly moved.

She then urged Cowasjee to expedite the closing of all his accounts so that they might start for America at an early date – but 'man proposes and God disposes' – this voyage was not destined to happen till many years later.

Her mother, who had been suffering for ten years from a chronic ailment was very poorly but Dosebai never thought that this illness might prove her last. Her illustrious mother died soon after Dosebai's return from her trip to Europe.

Preparatory to their departure for America, she decided to sell off the entire household effects including carriages, horses and even clothing and to let the two bungalows. As on the former occasion when she went to Delhi, her friends were put on the wrong scent by their giving out that this time, they were going to the Nilgiris (mountains in South India) for four years. Natives of India were opposed to the idea of selling household furniture, regarding it as an ill omen but she had no hesitation in disposing of their old wares to substitute new ones when required. However, all this excitement had to be put on hold for a few years as the little complications of life took over.

In the year 1880, Lord Ripon arrived in Bombay as Governor-General of India, replacing Lord Lytton. His arrival was the occasion of another jolly time. Lord and Lady Lytton also soon arrived in Bombay from Calcutta, en route to England, and Dosebai was invited to the Dock Yard enclosure to wish them 'God speed'. On seeing her there, Lord and Lady Lytton came up, and with great cordiality, shook hands with her and Cowasjee, expressing their pleasure at seeing them again.

Life soon returned to normal and Dosebai was invited to several balls and parties at Government House. She and her husband went to a ball given by General Warre at his residence where they had the honour of being presented to Lord Ripon.

The Raja of Chota Udepur wanted to host a reception for Sir James Fergusson Governor of Bombay and for this purpose, he requested Dosebai to place the hall of her palatial residence at his disposal for a couple of hours. The Raja did not speak English, so Dosebai also offered to act as an interpreter. After the reception was over, the Raja and his several wives who had also come there thanked her heartily for her great help.

Some months after this she was present at an evening party at the Government House, when Lady Fergusson who sat beside her much admired the border of her sari. Dosebai told her it was her own work and offered to embroider a cap for Lady Fergusson's little son. This was most graciously accepted, and forthwith, Dosebai commenced the work and presented the cap personally a week later, to Lady Fergusson who received it with great pleasure.

Dosebai's happy life was not without its moments of sadness. Her daughter's husband went to London again, and there he opened the firm of Messrs. Cama Bros. Goolbai also left for England with her children. After her daughter's departure for England, Dosebai's mind was ill at ease for many months. The Indians considered the crow to be a bird of ill omen and Dosebai was not long in realising that this belief was not quite unfounded. One day, she was scared out of her wits by the terrible screech of a crow and she fully expected to hear some very bad news. The whole of her body began to shake through vague, undefined fears and unhappily, she soon found the prophecy fulfilled. She had the misfortune to receive the dreadful news of her dear son-in-law's death in Davos-Platz, Switzerland, on 2nd January 1884, separated from his friends and relatives. (We later discovered that he had gone to Switzerland to seek a cure for tuberculosis. The Sanatorium at Davos-Platz was recommended). After a few months, her daughter returned to Bombay with her three grown-up children but, understandably, after the sad bereavement she had undergone, Goolbai's attitude to life was changed and desperately negative.

Goolbai also bade adieu to this world at Bandra (Bombay), on the 6th January 1890. It is needless to add that her death was another heavy blow for her parents.

During Dosebai's visit to Europe on the occasion of the Paris Exhibition, the thought of Cowasjee not sharing her pleasure often troubled her mind but she drew consolation from the prospect that they would make another trip together. She did make another, and most spectacular trip, but not with her husband for he too, had bidden farewell to this mortal world by that time.

Mr. Cowasjee Jehangir Jessawalla was born on 15th May 1819, immediately after the establishment of British Rule in Bombay. Even in those early days he had received an English education, which proved of the greatest use to him in the management of his father's firms, known in Northern India and Kabul under the name of Messrs. Jehangir and Co., which he was called upon to undertake as soon as he was seventeen. Travelling in those days was so very unsafe, troublesome and perilous that only a few hardy types could carry on and succeed in a business such as he conducted.

He established several firms in Northern India - in Peshawar, Rawalpindee, Murree Hill, Sukkar, Mooltan, Lahore and last but not least, Kabul itself, for the purpose of providing the British Army with supplies. (Pakistan, of course, did not exist in those days and India had a border with Afghanistan). He was held in high respect by many British officers of the Army and was, on one occasion, in

1848, presented with a '*Khillat*' (an award of honour), in the court of the Nawab of Bhawalpore. He was for several years, connected with the *Times of India* and worked as a guarantee broker for the well-known European firm of Messrs. Volkart Brothers for nearly 20 years, during which period he took a very active part in establishing many public companies such as the Bombay Native Insurance Company and the Bombay Oil Press Company. He also had his own steamers running between Bombay and Kathiawar. After leaving the firm of Messrs. Volkart Bros, he was employed as a broker in the firm of Messrs. Knoop and Company.

On the 4th December 1900 at the patriarchal age of 81, Cowasjee breathed his last leaving Dosebai, her sons and numerous other relatives to bemoan his loss. The extreme grief that she felt at heart can be better imagined than described. His soul left the terrestrial abode to choose a celestial residence, but the noble qualities of head and heart, which had endeared him to everyone, would never be obliterated from the minds of those who knew him. She loved him very much and always looked upon him as the inspirer of all that is good, noble and beautiful.

The intensity of grief began to tell on her health, and she was advised to remove to a temperate climate for a change. She therefore went first to Kashmir and then to South India and although the beauties of nature and change of air had their effect in lifting her spirits for a time, that venerable image of purity and nobility was never for a moment absent from her heart, causing occasionally a renewal of grief, which could not be mitigated except by the lapse of time.

Her youngest stepson, Dorabjee, who had his business in Srinagar (Kashmir), invited her to come to the north for a holiday. With her younger son Jamsetjee, she left in the beginning of May for Rawalpindee. It was a far cry from Bombay to Pindee, a distance of some 2000 miles, and they were four weary days and five consecutive nights in the train. After a short stay in Pindee, they proceeded by tonga (horse and carriage) to Srinagar, a drive of 200 miles, halting at *Dak* Bungalows at Murree, Baramulla, Dulai, Uri and other places. These were Government rest houses meant for touring officers and also for the use of the postal messengers, running or riding out with the Post (*Dak*) night and day. This postal system was replaced after the railways were built, around 1860 onwards.

Though the journey was tiring, it was a pleasant drive through mountainous regions with gloriously coloured foliage and walnut groves and avenues upon the banks of the Vale of Kashmir. The scenery was indescribable. The romances of Moore in the '*Lalla Rookh*' may be extravagant but after all, few will deny that fiction is not surpassed by fact. Srinagar was on an elevation of nearly 6000 ft above sea level and the final day's drive opened fantastic views before their eyes. Before reaching Srinagar, they entered Poplar Avenue, which was a unique sight and it resembled the long avenue of high grown trees she saw at Windsor when going to the Mausoleum. They reached their destination safe and in good health though completely exhausted. They stayed in a large wooden building containing the business and residential quarters of her stepson and his partners, carrying on their trade under the firm of Pestonjee and Son, General Merchants. It was situated on the riverbank in the midst of the commercial part of the city. For a few days the weather was rainy and they felt the cold so bitterly that they confined themselves to their quarters. The change in climate, however, brought great relief and Dosebai's health was considerably improved. It was a pity that the cherished desire to visit Kashmir was attained under such sad circumstances.

Srinagar was called the Venice of India. Most of the people lived in houseboats and all the buildings were surrounded by water. Kashmir was under the benign reign of Maharaja Partap Singh, assisted by his able and learned councillors. It was encouraging to observe that her stepson and many other Parsis were flourishing as merchants, doing business under the special patronage of His Highness. Dosebai had a leisurely time being taken around the beautiful Lake Dal in a boat and visiting the various parks and gardens. Srinagar was a popular resort for the British who would, occasionally, escape the extreme heat and discomfort of Delhi. It was also a most important trading post and of great commercial value to India.

Dosebai noted that although education had been freely introduced amongst the male sex in Kashmir and that almost all the high officials from the Prime Minister downwards were men of great culture, education amongst women had not made any advancement in such a well-refined state. This being the case, she did not have the opportunity of making the personal friendship of the ladies of the upper circle.

Her son, being familiar with the Royal household, wished to introduce her to His Highness the Maharaja and his Royal Ladies. But she was informed that the Royal Ladies had not returned from Jammu to Srinagar. His Highness, however, expressed his willingness to see them at his Palace and sent his own boat to escort them. On mooring at the Palace they were met by a Secretary who took them up a grand flight of stairs to a landing place and into the Grand Hall in the presence of His Highness. They found him seated on a white sheet of cloth spread out on the floor. On seeing them he got up at once and shook hands with them warmly. He ordered chairs to be brought for them but paying due homage to his exalted position, they humbly declined to sit on the chairs and asked to be allowed to take their seats on the same cloth on which His Highness was sitting. He was dressed so plainly in white that it reminded Dosebai of His Holiness Pope Leo XIII, who was all simplicity and preferred not to display his high position. They were introduced to the high officials, his brother amongst them to whom they subsequently paid a visit, at his own palatial residence.

During the conversation His Highness touched on many aspects of Dosebai's career, since he had come to know about it from his Secretary. The conversation turned to her education, her travels, and last but not least, her ascent in the balloon. Then he asked her whether she would have the same pluck and courage to repeat the feat again if he prepared a balloon at his own expense to which she very sensibly, answered in the negative. The interview was a very happy one, and lasted for over an hour. She earnestly thanked His

154

Highness for all his kindness and on her leaving, he offered a tray of leaves and betelnuts as the formal parting ceremony observed by the host to his guests.

They generally spent their evenings in boats across the Dal Lake, an immense stretch of water covered in many places with great lotus leaves and pink blossoms. Kashmir was very famous for fabulous fruit and vegetables. Big baskets of yellow pears, peaches and grapes as well as cauliflowers, tomatoes and many other vegetables were brought to them at all times of the day, for a few pennies. It was a land of ideal climate and stupendous scenery, where one might enjoy one's life upon a mere nothing, roaming over the Vale of Kashmir and its glorious mountains from April to November.

A site well worth visiting was the hill known as 'Solomon's Throne' or 'Takht-i-Suleman', from the top of which a beautiful, panoramic view of the city could be had. The city was a somewhat confused mass of houses overhanging either side of the river and the smaller canals, which in many places formed the only streets. The wooden houses, stained and weathered into rich tones of grey and brown, looked remarkably picturesque with their balconies and carved windows. The simple bridges across the river were built of beams laid on timber and stone piers.

They made an interesting excursion to 'Islamabad'. (Not to be confused with the present Islamabad in Pakistan). For this trip, they engaged a houseboat, called a '*doonga*' or '*kishtie*', which were numerous in Kashmir. Leaving Srinagar in the morning, they were soon gliding between banks covered with evergreen trees. When it grew dark they passed several other '*doongas*' and the crew in some of them were singing weird chants of which they seemed very fond. Next morning they were at 'Islamabad'. Here, they saw two impressive waterfalls cascading down the mountain with crystal clear water. The stunning scenery surpassed everything she had come across during her extensive travels in the East and West. After spending a week in the *doonga* they returned to Srinagar. One might easily spend a whole summer in this way on the Jhelum River and its tributaries, under the hospitable shade of a *doonga* making as many expeditions as one might fancy.

Little did Dosebai know, that many years later, her great grand-daughter, Mani Cama, would make a journey to Kashmir, too. Here is the story of this amazing trip. In 1933, when my mother (Mani Cama) was seventeen and had just passed her driving test, her father (Dosebai's grandson) retired from service in the Customs and Excise Department. His wife, Tehmina, promptly suggested that they all drive up to Srinagar in the mountain state of Kashmir, high up in the Himalayas. She thought it would be a fantastic family adventure to live on a houseboat for a couple of months on the stunningly beautiful Lake Dal, surrounded by the fabulous gardens laid out by the Mughal Emperors over 300 years earlier. Although Kashmir was about 2,500 miles away from Poona, the distance did not worry my grandmother. There were several drivers in the family and they could all take turns. There would be seven of them travelling – my grandmother (Mama), my grandfather (Papa), Uncle Pilloos (who was a bit of a mystery character who lived with the family, was very rich and had a stammer), my mother, her brother Naval who was an expert mechanic and their two younger sisters who, I imagine, had been excused from school.

This being such a grand and courageous (if not foolhardy), undertaking, meticulous details had to be worked out. Roads were unmade and almost non-existent, there were no petrol stations or service stops on the way and certainly no pubs to take a break in. The plan was to camp overnight, but not camping the way we know it. To start with, they bought a brand new 7-seater Hudson car from Ms. Kandawalla & Co., the biggest car dealers in those days. It was fitted out with special boxes, roof racks, plenty of spare tyres, tubes and all the mechanical equipment they might need. Also rifles and shotguns, which were *de rigeur* as hunting game was quite acceptable, not to mention the bandits they might meet along the way.

For the camping equipment another large vehicle was specially constructed for them – a customized van on an old Dodge chassis. This was fitted out with sleeping berths, water tanks and conveniences for overnight stays in the forests. Extra fuel would also have been carried somehow. Cooking utensils, huge quantities of tinned food, camping stoves, lanterns – just thinking about this makes me dizzy. It was a journey into the unknown. The driving was shared among Mama, Uncle Pilloos, my mother and Naval, as Papa did not drive. They had also chosen a delightful and strong Sikh driver to take charge of the van. His name was Avtar Singh. One sunny morning in March they set off.

In 1933 India was still under the British Raj and Pakistan did not exist. India was not one united country as it is today, but a collection of assorted states, some ruled directly by Indian rulers and some under British rule. There were even tiny city-states with very few inhabitants. The laws and customs of each state were different according to the religions and beliefs of the rulers. There were Hindu Rajas, Muslim Nawabs, Sikh Sardars and the like. Travellers passing through had to observe and respect the laws of wherever they were.

In Hindu states beef was prohibited, as the cow was considered sacred, whilst in Muslim states pork was strictly taboo. At each border crossing, the Customs guards checked the labels on each can of food (mostly imported from England) and simply destroyed whatever was not allowed. One could lose one's entire food supply this way, so, having wised up to this fact earlier, they removed all the labels from all the tins. This made for some interesting meals but at least they still had something left to eat!

One morning, they saw a beautiful peacock in a deserted clearing in the forest, just outside a village. Naval decided he would shoot it and they could have it for dinner. So he took a pot shot, missed, and the next thing they saw was a large crowd of angry villagers charging at them waving sticks and baying for their blood. The peacock is also a sacred bird (and even if it wasn't, how daft can you be?) So the family found themselves in big trouble. Luckily for them, their gallant Sikh driver came to the rescue and calmed the villagers down. They never found out what he said to them but it worked and they managed to drive away unharmed. This was a very close call.

They continued on their amazing journey north, driving through various cities, villages and thick forest. There were several punctures to contend with thanks to the numerous metal 'shoes' from the bullock carts that used the same tracks, and the odd mechanical breakdown. Now and again they would stop at a '*Dak*' bungalow.

The '*Dak*' bungalows were always in the middle of nowhere, surrounded by forests and wild animals. Light was provided by kerosene lamps and bath water heated on log fires. I have nostalgic memories of staying in them when we accompanied my father on one of his field trips. The smell of wood smoke and the kerosene lamps brings back warm, happy days.

I do not have a detailed diary of this historic journey but can only guess at their route north. They would have travelled via Ahmadabad to Jodhpur in Rajasthan and continued through wild country alternating between forests rich with game and dry stony desert with very little civilization and a few goats for company. Bikaner would have been on their route and almost certainly Rawalpindi, as that is where Grandmother was born. Here the true account continues – on virtually unmade mountain roads in hostile conditions they headed for the North-West Frontier and the infamous Khyber Pass.

This Pass in the Himalayas has been the gateway into India for umpteen raiders, marauders, conquerors and settlers from various regions of Central Asia and Europe over thousands of years – Alexander the Great and the many Mughal Emperors to name a few. It is now a corridor between Afghanistan and Pakistan, and just as dangerous and unpredictable as it has always been. As Pakistan did not exist in 1933, the border was guarded by Indian troops.

On reaching the North West Frontier, they were surrounded by wild looking Afridy tribesmen, brandishing rifles and bristling with loaded cartridge belts, not to mention the curved daggers on their hips. However, they were not as threatening as they looked and, under the watchful eyes of the Indian soldiers (Jawans), they crowded round the Hudson car patting its polished surface and poking its fat tyres. Silent and suspicious, their manners changed

158

instantly when Grandfather asked if they were in 'Pakhtoonistan,' which was the name they dearly desired to call this area if ever they were granted independence. The magic word brought smiles and gestures of friendship but one did not wish to push one's luck. The family posed for photographs with the Jawans, and Uncle Pilloos tried to impress the tribesmen that he was a VIP while twirling his impressive moustache. With a prudent hint from the Army Corporal not to linger amongst these unpredictable firebrands, they turned back and headed for Murree on the way to Srinagar. The Murree Pass leads directly to Srinagar and forms part of the line dividing present day India and Pakistan.

Thus they entered Srinagar. The sight that greeted them was spectacular. There were vast gardens and canals laid out for miles and miles. Designed by Persian architects commissioned by the great Mughal Emperors of India in the 16th and 17th Centuries, they were primarily laid out as pleasure playgrounds and summer retreats for the Royals to escape the unbearable heat of Delhi and the plains. However, there was a practical use for this, too. When the ice of the Himalayan mountain range melted in summer, it opened the roads for raiders, freebooters, Afridy tribesmen and even organised armies from the north to pour into Kashmir and grab this lovely land. So the Mughal Kings discreetly moved their armies to these summer frontiers while ostentatiously holidaying in this paradise.

Paradise no doubt it was, as any visitor even today would testify. It was 400 years ago that a court poet composed the immortal lines *'Agar behesht ber rue zamin hast, hamin hast, hamin hast, hamin hast'* – 'If Paradise be on the face of this Earth, this is it, this is it, this is it'. These words are carved into a marble tablet in the Royal Court at Agra, but refer to Srinagar.

The most pleasurable pursuit in Srinagar was living in a houseboat, on the great Dal Lake and moving from place to place as you pleased. It was exciting to be in a floating home, complete with bedrooms, kitchen and bath, lazing on rich Persian carpets on the verandahs while gliding majestically on the lake or down one of the quiet canals that formed a labyrinth around the lake. Or you could stay put in some shady bower of your choice for days on end as the icy cold waters of the Himalayas flowed past.

The British introduced the houseboat lifestyle. A Hindu Maharaja ruled this province and he would not permit any outsiders to own land or build houses in Kashmir. The British visitors respected this ruling but cleverly circumvented the law by building floating houses on the water.

The houseboat this family rented was called 'The Lion's Lair' and it was their home for two months. It was owned by an enterprising man called Rahim Khan who was friend, philosopher, cook and butler with enough experience to handle the eccentricities of visitors from all parts of the world. He produced magnificent meals cooked on board with the freshest ingredients. Imagine the ecstasy of lying on cushions on a moonlit night on the lake, surrounded by water lilies and listening to the water lapping the side of the boat.

Native Kashmiris had an amazing capacity to withstand the cold. They had to live here long after the tourists had gone back to warmer climes and the lake was freezing over. No central heating and not much shelter in a wooden hut. But their ingenuity knew no bounds and they tied earthen pots filled with hot coals round their stomachs, which kept their entire systems warm. During summer, however, hordes of them would jump into the icy cold water early every morning for their daily baths. My grandmother, ever adventurous and thinking 'how bad could that be' got it into her head to try the same. One morning the family awoke to find her in her swimming costume ready for a dip. They watched in disbelief as she jumped in nonchalantly as the rest of them shivered in horror. Needless to say, she waded out as fast as she had entered with 'never again' written all over her face. But she did it!

The time came to leave Paradise and go home. I am grateful that someone took the trouble to write an account of what must have been an epic adventure so that I could share it with you. It is also wonderful that Dosebai wrote her memoirs so many years before this, or we would never have had any record of her travels, either!

CHAPTER 23

TRAVELS IN SOUTH INDIA

In the year 1904, now aged 73, Dosebai lost her only beloved grand-daughter, Ratanbai Patell, who tragically died of plague at the age of 33, leaving one son and daughter to bemoan her loss. The calamity told so seriously upon Dosebai's health that she was again compelled to leave her home for a long change. Having been advised to avail herself of a cold climate she resolved to go to Ootacamund in the Nilgiri Hills. She set off in the middle of October with her younger son Jamsetjee and a servant, for Madras (now Chenai). After arriving at Raichur, the junction for the Madras Railway they proceeded to Madras, a distance of about 800 miles which they reached in the early morning after several hours travel by train.

The intention was to proceed to the Nilgiri Hills from Bombay via Madras but their friends strongly recommended them to visit Pondicherry so they decided to go there first. The train journey took them through broad, green, rice fields covered with water. In the distance, they could see the blue Arcot Hills but the frequent groves of palm trees along the route bore testimony to their being very near the sea. The further they travelled, the richer became the soil. At noon, they arrived at Vellapuram Junction, where they changed carriages for Pondicherry and after an hour's run, the train drew up at the station where they were surrounded by Customs officials who examined their luggage with such scrutiny that not a single piece of cloth was left unturned. (Pondicherry was a little French enclave in British India).

Soon afterwards they found themselves being transported rapidly through the main street in a *'pousse-pousse'*. It was a sort of perambulator and one felt as if one were being wheeled down the street in the days of childhood. It was a comfortable conveyance,

161

made no noise and was swift but safe. Horse carriages were almost absent here and the noiseless traffic was one of the charms of the French capital. It was said about the *'pousse-pousse'* man that he neither 'kicked nor shied'. After a short ride they found themselves at Sooboo's Hotel, which was worthy to be compared with any in Europe.

Pondicherry could well be called a paradise for a poor man. The balconies with their ornate balustrades overhanging the streets looked rather picturesque and with its elegant and architectural yet shabby-chic buildings, it was all undeniably French. In the evening after a short rest, they left the hotel and walking a few yards came to the *Place de la Republique* where, on a pedestal stood the statue of Dupleix, the great French General. A few yards from the statue was Government House and on the other side there was a public bandstand where people took an evening stroll and enjoyed the music. There were many legendary stories about the Generals of olden days fighting hand to hand in southern parts of India to establish the supremacy of their respective powers – the French, the Dutch, the English and the Marathas. It was said by an English author that Pondicherry was like a football, kicked about from the French to the Dutch, from the Dutch to the French and during the scrimmage, between the French and the English.

This was a nice, quiet and cheap place for retired people to live in most comfortably. On their rambles here, they made friends with two Parsi gentlemen who were connected with the Rodier Mill. This was one of the oldest fabric mills in India and is still in existence as Anglo-French Textiles. In Pondicherry, thanks to the French connection, wines such as champagne, claret and cognac were available at a very low price, so much so that people could afford to drink champagne at every meal. After passing ten merry days in the French town, which served as an historical relic of an Empire in India that was destroyed before it was securely built, they proceeded to the next stage of their journey.

Leaving Pondicherry, they took a train heading for the Nilgiri Hills. They had to change trains at the junction of Mettapalum, where they entered a narrow gauge and really wonderful train to go up to the heights. The hills rose to an elevation of 6,500 feet. Their luggage had to be tied securely on the top of the train or else it would roll about and was in danger of landing up in the valley below. As the train had to go up a very steep climb, it had strong pulley brakes fixed to it; but that was no guarantee that it would not roll backwards and cause an accident of a serious nature, to put it mildly. Travelling up the hills, they enjoyed exceedingly beautiful (and very English) scenery as far as Coonoor. The higher they went, the more afraid they were of being thrown down into the deep valley should anything go wrong with the train. They came across several wooden bridges on the way and wondered how they must have been built. In fact – the whole Railway line excited their admiration at the engineering skill displayed in the construction of it. From Coonoor, the journey was made by *tonga* and the drive was not very interesting, as on each side of the road one saw nothing but thick avenues of high trees. However, on reaching their destination, the lovely Ootacamund, they were stunned by the sweeping and bright green vistas of the tea plantations that greeted them.

Immediately on their arrival, they went straight to a Parsi shop-keeper, Mr. Hazari, a very old inhabitant who lived here with his big family. They made some inquiries for residential quarters, but he and his family would not allow them to go anywhere that evening, and extended their hospitality. With great appreciation, they put up at his house with his big family. As the fatigue of the journey from Coonoor told in some measure upon Dosebai's health, she had to keep indoors the next day but on the following day they went out with Mr. Hazari, to find some accommodation. They found a beautiful house, which belonged to an English widow. The house was located on top of a hill from where there was a commanding view of the city. Dosebai liked the house but as they were now on an elevation of 6,500 ft. above the sweltering plain, she felt the place cold and windy but this drawback was remedied by keeping the mantle lamps always lit, which warmed the place up. The climate being congenial and the air cool, crisp and fresh, they rapidly gained in health and strength.

Eucalyptus trees were very common in Ooty and rows of them were to be seen growing on both sides of the road. They saw the ostentatious palaces of the Maharaja of Mysore and the Gaekwar of Baroda, the Library, the Assembly rooms and, of course, Government House. The racecourse had a lovely outlook and the band generally played here and also at the Botanical gardens, which were full of beautiful plants, shrubs and flowers. The gardens were lush with lovely roses and great bushes of fragrant geraniums, which filled the air with their delicious scent. Gardening in the Nilgiris was a pleasure, as the seeds and plants grew rapidly as if by magic. Vegetables too, grew with great vigour. Many permanent European residents and enterprising Indians kept thriving kitchen gardens from which they supplied the market or, as it was called, 'Shandy', which took place once a week. On 'Shandy Day' one was expected to purchase all his or her provision of meat, poultry, vegetables, eggs, grains and other essentials for the week, unless one wished to pay three times the price for the same thing on other days of the week. The Shandy Bazaar was one of the most colourful and attractive sights of Ooty. However, *Shandy Day* was a trial for every household, as the cooks and servants spent hours there and invariably returned home completely drunk.

There was a sect of herdsmen called *'Todas'*, which were the most intriguing of all the Nilgiri Hill tribes. The only aborigines of these hills, being tall and athletic with strong, sinewy limbs, they were a striking race. They were good looking and some of the women were really pretty, having fine eyes, black hair and skins of ivory fairness. Their dress was peculiar, consisting of a single woollen mantle. The *Todas* lived in hamlets called *'Mands'* which consisted of two or three oval huts with a low entrance or doorway hardly two feet in height, closed inside by a sliding block of wood. They crawled in and out of their huts on hands and knees. Being full of superstitions, they were a gentle, laid-back race, the main occupation being cattle herding. Their diet consisted of milk, ghee and a little corn. They also practiced polyandry – a woman marrying all the brothers of one family. (Don't ask).

Wherever Dosebai went, she found friends. This was possibly because there were enterprising Parsis everywhere. Mr. Kenny was the most popular Parsi gentleman living here for many years on the recommendation of his Doctor. She had known him years ago in Bombay. His business in Bombay, Messrs. Kenny and Co., was still flourishing. They were dealers in jewellery, clocks and Swiss watches. On hearing of her arrival, he and Mrs. Kenny called on Dosebai, He was an Honorary Magistrate, a member of the Ooty Municipality and respected by all. They had a magnificent house, where they held frequent 'at-home' parties. There were Lawn Tennis courts in the midst of their beautiful garden, where most of the ladies and gentlemen who knew the game enjoyed it heartily, while others delighted in strolling on the lawns, playing croquet and taking part in pleasant conversations. Dosebai's stay in Ooty lasted for nearly a month and a half and the bracing climate did wonders to restore her old spirit.

She took leave of Ooty at the end of November and proceeded to Bangalore. Bangalore was known for its dry climate and it was for this reason, popular as a health resort. Living was comparatively cheap and any amount of green vegetables and fruit could be had. True to form, here she renewed the friendship of her old friends Mr. and Mrs. Bhabha, for many years residents of that city. They were often invited to tea and dinner and went for drives together. Mr. Bhabha held the very important post of Director of Public Instruction in Mysore State and carried much influence in the territory. Mrs. Bhabha moved in the best English society and through her, Dosebai had the pleasure of making the acquaintance of Mr and Mrs. Armrod. Mr. Armrod was the Editor of a well-known Bangalore newspaper and they became good friends.

During Dosebai's visit, the future King George V and Queen Mary, then on a tour of India as the Prince and Princess of Wales, paid a visit to Bangalore. It had been decided that His Royal Highness should perform the unveiling ceremony of a statue of the late beloved Empress Queen Victoria. A large *mandap* (stage), adorned with buntings of various colours, was erected to hold the distinguished gathering invited to witness the interesting ceremony.

Through the kindness of Mr. Bhabha, Dosebai and her son had invitations to be present. They went along with Mrs. Bhabha and were able to secure front row seats in the *mandap*. Being quite close to the scene of ceremony they commanded a very nice view of all that transpired on the occasion, and could clearly see the beaming faces of Their Royal Highnesses. They returned home delighted at being able to have been there.

Mr. Bhabha insisted that they should visit the Kolar Gold Mines, one of the best attractions to be seen by a visitor to Bangalore and Mysore. He gave them a letter to the Chief of one of the best mines, requesting him to show them everything worth seeing. As Mrs. Bhabha had promised to join them, they were all the more encouraged to go. Arriving at the Gold Mine station at about eleven o'clock, to their great delight they were soon in the agreeable company of the Chief, who had come in person to receive them. He drove them straight to the *dak* bungalow, which was situated on an elevation, from where they could see the different mills while seated on the veranda. The Chief then took them to see the different departments of the mill and the machinery with which gold was extracted and brought into use. They were awe-struck when they realised the various and hugely complicated processes that were employed to remove the gold from the quartz ore. Well-known writers, in praise of these gold mines, had written much, and they really were worth a visit. They returned to the station late in the evening, accompanied by the Chief, and went back to Bangalore by the evening train.

Next on the agenda was Mysore, where some very interesting sights and aspects of Indian life were to be seen. Their Royal Highnesses had just recently left the city, which had not yet lost its excitement. Since Mrs. Bhabha had kindly addressed a letter to the Manager of a well-known hotel in Mysore owned by a Parsi gentleman who was living here with his large family (sounds familiar), the latter was good enough to be present at the station to receive them and drive them to the hotel. All the roads looked bright and attractive with beautiful *mandaps*, buntings, flags and various other brilliant decorations, which had not yet been removed after the

166

Royal visit, and thus they were lucky enough to see the preparations made in Mysore for the reception of their noble guests.

The following day the Manager took them to see Seringapatam, famous for its dreadful siege. They saw countless tombs on both sides of the road of valiant heroes who had fought bravely in honour of the British flag during the siege, and in whose memory a beautiful pillar had been erected. Their carriage approached the glorious memorial building through an exuberant and picturesque garden. Inside, the walls were painted with views of the horrific battle between the British troops and Hyder Ali and Tipoo Sultan. In spite of the depressing theme, they were so wonderfully painted that one could not help admiring them. This square two storeyed building inside which there were several staircases leading to small rooms with prettily carved windows, was called 'Tipoo's place of Rendezvous'. A cool breeze soothed them gently and after a little picnic, they proceeded on their march to see the Mausoleum of Hyder Ali and Tipoo Sultan, the famous Muslim heroes and warriors, situated in the Lal Bagh. Before entering they passed through an imposing arch, on which there were a number of platforms, on which Indian musicians performed with drums on important holidays. The Mausoleum was a handsome square pavilion of marble, surmounted by a dome with graceful minarets at its four angles and surrounded by beautiful columns of black hornblende. The ornately carved double doors were inlaid with ivory and led to the marble tombs, within which lay the warriors. The tombs bore inscriptions in verse, recording their deaths as noble martyrs.

Returning to Bombay with batteries recharged, Dosebai set about planning her next adventure.

167

CHAPTER 24

DOSEBAI'S SECOND VOYAGE TO ENGLAND AND SUBSEQUENT TOUR ROUND THE WORLD

In the year 1906, having sold a portion of her Bombay property at a reasonably good price, she resolved to make a second voyage to England, and sailed for London in the middle of May by the *S.S. Yarra.*

She disembarked at Marseilles, proceeded to London by rail, and took up her residence at 'Batliboi House', 16 Trebovir Road, Earl's Court – a newly opened Parsi house kept by an old acquaintance. This was a most desirable haven for a stranger in a foreign land as it brought her into immediate touch with her own countrymen and women, even though most of them were young students. What gave her most delight on this occasion was to meet in London, her best and oldest friend, Mrs. Ahlers, whom she had not seen for 28 years.

Also, India's foremost politician, Mr. Dadabhoy Naorojee, who had known her family from infancy, was residing at Balham with his granddaughters and grandson. At his suggestion, she moved to that more suburban – and therefore quieter – part of the Metropolis. She stayed here for three months, and Mr. Dadabhoy – the Grand Old Man of India as he was called – despite his patriarchal age, astonished her by the energy and enthusiasm with which he still continued to work for the good of India and its millions of poverty-stricken people. He even contemplated re-entering British Parliament, and never allowed despondency to get the better of his optimism.

Her stay in England was destined to be brief, and September found her returning to Bombay, for reasons partly climatic and partly domestic. Home again, she found herself once more in the midst of her family and friends and acting on their advice, she now determined to part with the rest of her property, comprising of land and three buildings. A newly formed company called the Zoroastrian Building Society made her an adequate offer and she soon found herself freed from the cares and worries of managing a big estate in her old age. Meanwhile, it was agreed that the purchase money should be paid by instalments and as the property was being acquired for a good and charitable purpose, she readily consented. She even attended the ceremony of laying the foundation stone of the building about to be erected on part of the site of her late property. For that purpose, an auspicious day was chosen, - *Jamshedi Navroz* – which fell on March 21st 1907. (The Spring Equinox and the natural start of the New Year). The longest lane has a turning, and her patience was rewarded by the purchase-money being all paid by the 15th of May the same year and the deed of sale fully executed.

During this time, she made preparations for a tour around the world, along with both her sons. Her intention thus to become a globe-trotter, at the age of 76, naturally aroused not a little interest amongst her friends and well-wishers in Bombay and she received a good deal of attention from the English and Bombay papers.

Dosebai and her sons set sail for Yokohama in the P & O Steamship *'Delta'* on May 29th 1907– Royal Oak Day – the English called it, and when the ship reached the open sea, it made for Colombo. According to Indian tradition, she made a 'peace offering' to the sea of sugar, coconut and flowers, and took a last long, lingering look at Bombay with its magnificent harbour and busy wharves and its amphitheatre of distant hills in the background – a truly sublime spectacle. Ten miles away from the Prince's Dock – their point of embarkation – they passed the Lighthouse, and there the harbour pilot left them, handing them over to the care of the Captain of the *'Delta'*.

They spent most of their time between meals on the promenade deck and as they were a small but select party, they all got along very well. There were fifteen of them including the doctor, a lively and amiable young man who was, of course, indispensable on board a ship.

On the morning of June 1st, after one or two signs that the monsoon was about to burst, they arrived safely at Colombo, the capital and chief seaport of Ceylon (now Sri Lanka). Colombo was remarkable for its fine cinnamon, cloves, its coastal beauty and its world famous jewels. There were electric trams plying the fine broad streets giving quite an air of modernity to this city of the Far East. Here too, all outgoing steamers stopped and so it was a port of call for all nations. As the interval of stay was short, they could not avail themselves of the opportunity of seeing Colombo thoroughly.

Before leaving Colombo for Singapore, the outward English mails were taken on board from another steamer that came direct from Marseilles and some twenty more passengers joined them, the most important amongst them being the Chinese Ambassador and his entourage returning from London. That very modern accessory the Gramophone, also appeared on board and they formed quite a lively and in many ways, very interesting party.

On June 6th, six days after leaving Colombo they sighted Penang as its lofty and evergreen mountains burst refreshingly upon the horizon. Originally a penal settlement, Penang was now a popular health resort with a luxuriantly tropical but salubrious climate and a thriving commerce. Its other name was Prince of Wales Island, and the electric tram was an institution here, too. One of the finest sights in Penang was the waterfall situated in the public gardens, four miles away in the midst of verdant vegetation. Endless avenues of coconut trees were a prominent feature of this part of the Peninsula and the drives to and fro were exceedingly pleasant.

There was however, a great drawback to a voyage by a mail steamer. It did not remain long at any port of call and therefore it would have been better to go on a tour of this kind on a regular passenger steamer. However, Singapore was the next port of call and the voyage there was delightful. The Straits of Malacca were very narrow and the land on both sides was perilously close to the ship.

They admired the Captain's skill in navigating and it was an exciting experience, never to be forgotten.

The voyage from Penang to Singapore was short and sweet. It so happened that many passengers proposed to disembark at Singapore, and it occurred to some of them to give a concert on board – a treat that was much appreciated. Another pleasant diversion was the taking of photographs in a group, for which they had to thank Lieutenant Lindsay, who had voyaged with them from Bombay.

The closer they got to Singapore, the narrower the approach channel became, so much so that they felt as if they were passing through streets or gardens. Entering the harbour, they observed that the overlooking hills almost exactly resembled Bombay's Cumballa or Malabar Hills, even to the flagstaff on the summit signalling the arrival of their steamer. Upon arrival, they were fortunate in being chaperoned round the town by Dosebai's sons' friend, Mr. H.P. Kaka. Dosebai found Singapore very modern, indeed. It was, amongst other things, the rendezvous and coaling station of the British India Squadron and in the extent of trade carried on with other parts of the world, it was of paramount importance.

It was a fairly speedy goodbye to Singapore. Admittedly, they steamed away in the mist and rain but happily, they had escaped the much dreaded monsoon and reached Hong Kong in fair weather.

Here, as at Colombo, Penang and Singapore, the harbour bar was a splendid sight, with its sailing ships, steamers and local small craft of every description and its constant activity. It was a blending of impregnable strength and picturesque beauty. Behind the harbour rose the hills, semi-circular in shape, the sublimely lofty peaks protecting the town, whose double name reminded them of China and 'The Empire upon which the sun never sets' – to wit – Hong Kong and Victoria.

Boarding a steam launch kindly supplied by their good skipper Captain Daniel, they reached the King Edward Hotel owned *naturellement*, by a Parsi gentleman. The Parsis were incredibly enterprising, and had businesses in every part of the globe that the

British had spread their influence. For such a small community, this was very much to their credit. To Dosebai's enormous delight, the proprietors of the hotel also supplied them with Parsi dinners. They met several other Parsis, amongst them the head of Petit's Firm, Mr. Sethna, who was here doing business in Bombay yarn, and Sir Hormusjee N. Mody, carrying on an extensive exchange business with almost all the leading banks of Hong Kong. The latter gentleman invited them to stay in his palatial residence, but she preferred to remain at the hotel, though she fully appreciated all the kindness extended to them. Beautiful Chinese vases and porcelain were offered to Dosebai by this amiable gentleman, but she had reluctantly and regretfully to decline the offer as she was travelling round the world, and could not see her way to carry these with her.

Before leaving, however, she made a tour of the shops in Queen's Road. This was the principal street and it was one of the most magnificent thoroughfares she had ever seen. Its shops, teeming with all manner of silver, silk, ivory, lacquer and porcelain goods, cedar wood ornaments, and other ornamental products of Chinese industry, were a sight which deeply impressed her, and she decided that Hong Kong took the premier place among the Far East colonies of the British Empire. Of course, the population was predominantly Chinese, but there were also some ten thousand Europeans, and the town itself rose terrace above terrace in ever-increasing beauty and splendour with, finally, a commanding view of the extensive harbour below. Here, Indian and Chinese merchants jostled each other in peaceful industrial rivalry, and the former took a lively interest in her tour round the world.

As to the transport, at the foot of the slope there were electric trams and further up, sedan chairs and that ubiquitous Eastern vehicle, the man-drawn 'Rickshaw'. Whilst here, she also visited the Victoria Park and this gave her the opportunity of seeing the 'Peak District' of the town, with its fine private residences and superb views from the Peak summit about 200 feet high. At night, the effect of a myriad lights from ships at anchor and of the flashes of electric searchlights was as if one were gazing at the starry heavens with meteors bursting at intervals across the stellar space, whilst in the daytime the busy traffic bristled with life and animation. Steam launches darted hither and thither amongst the bulkier steam and sailing vessels and the battleships of British build – like bulldogs of the deep – combined to form a maritime picture worthy of J.W. Turner. Dosebai praised the steeply inclined cable tramway from base to peak as a wonder of the great engineering skill of the mechanical age.

The view from Sir H. Mody's awesome residence was stupendous. They accepted an invitation to dinner and sat amidst wonders of the artistic and the antique in his lovely home, which was full of bespoke furniture, choice paintings and exquisite porcelain of Chinese make. The evening was reminiscent of her younger days, for life had brought sad bereavements and latterly she seldom attended such social gatherings in Bombay. At Sir Mody's that night, however, Dosebai seemed to live her young life again. She met, at the banquet, many English and Parsi friends and distinguished personages. With its countless electric lights, its superbly served dishes and its toasts – which last elicited a speech from herself, to the delight of the assembled guests – it was like a scene from the Arabian Nights. And so the evening passed, concluding with music and other entertainment.

On June 16th, another friend, Mr. Sorabji Sethna, invited them to take a trip to Macao, an old Portuguese town. It was also called the Monte Carlo of the East, with its ancient forts, gardens and grottoes. What Dosebai saw there in all their unholy evidence were gambling houses, frequented by Christian Europeans and Englishmen, and this on Sunday, of all days of the week. She was exceedingly shocked at this eye-opener. The next day, a *Daily Mail* reporter sought to draw her into a political discussion but she refused to be so drawn, and he confined the interview to her views on the advantages of travel. Imagine her surprise when, in the Hong Kong *Daily mail* of the morrow, her views appeared in print. These, the Bombay papers reproduced in still more glowing colours. These interviewers were so fond of colouring their copy, that she was compelled to point out certain discrepancies in their accounts. Not much has changed there, then!

Their friends drove them about the environs of the town, and also to the 'Happy Valley' Racecourse, an odd title for such an association of institutions, for the cemetery for all creeds and people was just opposite the racecourse. Here, in a Christian burial ground were monuments of all shapes and sizes and access to it was by means of steps surmounted by parapets, as it stood on the summit of the hill. Of special interest in this cemetery, for Dosebai, was the Parsi portion, beautifully laid out with flowers to make it look like a garden with a fountain playing in the midst.

Hong Kong was full of novelty and variety and an unusual feature of this island was the way in which its roads were laid out with one of them running the whole length of the island, some eleven or twelve miles. There was also the Botanical Garden and the magnificent aqueduct, about two miles in length. She paid a visit to the Chinese jewellery shops, where she bought a quantity of gold and silverware, including bracelets, caps, and table inkstands. They were also invited to the stately residence of Sir Paul Chaiter, a partner of her old friend Sir. H. Mody, who accompanied them to tea there. Sir Paul's residence was situated halfway up the Peak. It was a wonderful structure, almost a royal palace both without and within, with its pillars and staircase of sculpted marble and granite and its choice and rare collection of Chinaware – at least a million dollars worth.

They visited the kitchen-house, presided over by a Chinese chef who explained in detail all the many cooking contrivances, so intricately arranged as to disguise the fact that it was the culinary room of the mansion. Then they adjourned to the tearoom, and enjoyed in delicate china cups, the purest China tea. Sir Paul Chaiter insisted on presenting them with a box of tea of prime quality, and told them to drink it on their voyage as the tea provided on board was generally below par, even for first class passengers.

And now the time was drawing near for Dosebai to resume her journey. They were due to sail on June 24th and as they booked through the firm of Messrs. Thomas Cook and Son, everything was very well organised. The last two days – Saturday and Sunday –

were divided between a visit to their good friend, Sir H. Mody, and packing for departure. A final *Daily Mail* interview and soon they were leaving Hong Kong.

The Ernest Simmons

CHAPTER 25

BOUND FOR JAPAN

It was a French Steamer of the *Messageries Maritimes* – the *'Earnest Simmons'* – and Captain Gerard and his officers gave them a hearty welcome. The passengers responded by presenting each of them with a bouquet. The boat looked far superior to the *Delta,* the ship that had brought them to Hong Kong from Bombay. Not only was the décor and service much better, but also the food. Dosebai formed the opinion that the French were born cooks, more like Parsi cooks and so they made everything exactly to her taste. The English, she said, with all their good qualities, had not learnt the art of cooking and that is why, she supposed, London and the big cities used French or Swiss cooks and waiters in their restaurants, their hotels and in some private houses, too. (How things have changed today! The food capital of the world is now unanimously accepted to be London, with the whole world's cuisine available). Their ship was bound for Japan with Shanghai being the next port of call, and here they arrived after a pleasant voyage on June 27th. The vision of Hong Kong was still in her mind, with its houses perched on every available crag shoulder and its wonderful harbour, alive with sampans, junks and above all, bristling with masts 'majestically stern' by reason of the presence of British battleships.

Shanghai was the greatest commercial centre of China, but the harbour bar prevented the approach of big liners and so they had to enter it in smaller steamers. Passing up the river Wossung, the view of the line of factories, mills, wharves and warehouses and other buildings was a very imposing one and the huge fleet of junks lying off the native city was indeed, impressive to behold with the American, English and French settlements in their respective backgrounds. The Chinese tower of course, was the most prominent feature of the City.

Whilst staying in Shanghai, they visited Mr. and Mrs. Solina, her son's friends. They had already heard of Dosebai's coming, through the Bombay papers. They also met Mr. N. Tata, another friend of her elder son, the head of the Tata firm and a merchant of high standing, who had been apprised of their coming by Mr. N. Sethna of Hong Kong. Judge, dear reader, of her extreme delight in meeting old Parsi friends in far off Shanghai. Shanghai, by the way, was also called the Paris of the Far East, and the wealthy Mandarin merchants came here from the interior to spend their money and enjoy the pleasures of life. The Bund and the Maloo were the two principal highways and they stretched for miles with shops on each side full of all sorts of fancy goods.

On June 28th they set sail for Japan with very few passengers on board, yet with everything sumptuously provided both in the matter of food and entertainment. For the first day or two, they experienced a terrifying typhoon – a phenomenon common in the China seas – but then they reached Kobe, via Nagasaki, and entered the beautiful inland sea of Japan. This sea was really more like a strait or natural canal than a sea, being about 250 miles in length and universally admired for its loveliness – an archipelago of unsurpassed beauty and for a background, having mountains and scenic effects too glorious to describe. The blues, greens and turquoise of the islands and islets were a perfect study in colour and configuration, luxuriantly rich in cultivation and dotted with houses and temples and little villages, whilst junks plied to and fro upon the waters.

Having arrived at Kobe, it was comforting to know that her elder son was not altogether unacquainted with the town. In fact, they were once again in the midst of friends, and the drive through this centre of commerce along the Motomachi and to the Nanko Temple, was very enjoyable. It was a brief bright stay, an overnight call so to speak, and the next day they heaved anchor for Yokohama. Two of the passengers Dosebai met on board were particularly interesting – a French gentleman and his Japanese wife. They were a unique couple, both clever and very happy in each other's company. The lady, although Japanese, could speak English and French quite fluently and they had a little baby son – Dosebai was not familiar with the concept of mixed marriages, so she enjoyed conversing with them. When they reached Yokohama the entire population of the city seemed to be gathered on the landing stage and such a mixture of nationalities, too!

The Customs House officials, thanks to the friends who came to receive them, were satisfied as to their bona-fides and now they were in the 'Liverpool' of Japan, with its imposing Bund or Sea Wall front, on the way to Mr. Pestonjee's residence, where they were received by Mrs. Pestonjee, who bore the same name as Dosebai's late daughter, Goolbai. Their children, aged four and two respectively, spoke Japanese quite fluently but as the English language had common currency, there was no difficulty in making oneself understood. Yokohama was a cosmopolitan town, quite a European centre of the Far East though in other respects, strictly oriental, with its rickshaws drawn by human horses. In the gaiety and variety of its shops, it could well be likened to Paris and shopping here, as in the other big cities of Japan was terrific fun. All this wealth of art ware, curios and manufactured goods was the growth of only half a century – so rapid had been the development of Japan. Here was the famous Kana Koba, a bazaar of all sorts of fancy stalls, artistically arranged and full of fascination to the would-be purchaser. At night the brilliantly lit scene was enchanting and deliciously inviting.

The beautiful street of Benton Dori was the centre of their visit the following day, and here one was again lost in wonderment at the pictures and scenes painted on silk, the screens, the embroidery work, silk wares, lacquer work, carved ivory curios, porcelain and many other products of native art.

One morning, they set off for Tokyo to see the Exhibition there. In Hong Kong, they had been advised to take mineral baths in Japan, so their first thought, on reaching the capital, was to seek out Dr. Aoyama, the eminent physician. Finding him out on calling, they made an appointment for the next day. Meanwhile, they took up quarters at the Imperial Hotel, the grandest residence of its kind in Tokyo – a building like those one saw in England and on the

Continent. Tokyo had quite a look of modernity about it, with its gardens, avenues, electric lighting and street tram lines but it was also a city of temples; and here, of course, were all the Government Offices and last, but not least, the Mikado's Palace. There were plenty of American, European and English tourists with most of whom they were able to strike up an acquaintance and it was a golden opportunity to compare notes on their travel experiences.

The visit to Dr. Aoyama, the next morning, was purely a formal one and resulted in his advising them to take the recuperative baths at Atami, but they elected to remain in Tokyo; and after leaving the Doctor (to whom they spoke through an interpreter), they proceeded to the Exhibition in the Park. It was arranged in sections, the buildings being massive and impressive, and the exhibits altogether exquisite, especially the beautiful lacquer work in gold and silver – the pride and ornament of Japanese workmanship – and deservedly popular throughout the world. Europeans, Chinese and Japanese constituted the bulk of the visitors, but they also had the pleasure of meeting old friends, Mr. and Mrs. Lam; and Dosebai appreciated the fact that Parsis, both husbands and wives, had finally made a departure from the old traditional habit and now visited foreign lands together.

The visit to the Meiji Industrial Exhibition at Ueno Park in Tokyo was a revelation, for here they saw a wonderful blend of ancient and modern workmanship – antique models of temples and shrines – jostling side by side with the latest types of naval architecture and goods of all description, displayed in every variety of arrangement. This was an extravagant showcase of the blossoming of electric light in Tokyo. Near the main entrance, huge pots of roses and peonies were interwoven with around 300 light bulbs with a background of a 160 metre long purple and white wisteria enhanced with brilliant electric light. Then too, as though to remind them of London and its Earl's Court Exhibition, there was a giant Ferris Wheel and Merry-go-rounds, suggestive of the lighter side of life's experiences and of the truth that it takes all sorts and conditions to make a world. After a tour of the Exhibition with its wonderful wealth of bewilderingly magnificent exhibits, they returned to Yokohama by rail.

Here, on the 4th of July, they had the good fortune to be present at a time which coincided with the celebration by the Americans of the Independence Declaration Day, and their transatlantic friends had left nothing undone to make the display as imposing as possible. The ships in the harbour were gaily lit up and there was a pyrotechnic performance such as it would have been impossible to beat anywhere, for the Japanese and Chinese were past masters of the art. The Club Hotel, which faced the Bund, or Sea Wall afforded a splendid view of the proceedings and they were guests for the evening, their host and hostess having reserved a special room from which to view the fireworks and the procession of boats.

They then enjoyed the hot springs of Atami, whose situation was also very charming, with hills for a background and the sea in front. The town was reached from Yokohama, via Kodzee, and the journey was very pleasant, Nature having spread herself out like a garden with pretty villages dotted along the route. The last stage of the journey, after leaving Odawara, was accomplished in what was called a Trolley Car – drawn by coolies – human horses, as Dosebai called them, running along metre-gauge rails by the side of the sea. The road itself was hewn out of the mountainside for a distance of some fifteen miles and went through delightfully picturesque scenery, with constantly changing views and was at a good height above sea level. And the incredible *Coolies!* They were fine, tall, stalwart fellows and down the sloping portion of the journey, they ran at high speed, so that it needed but little exercise of imagination to fancy themselves in a railway carriage, the cars themselves being closed but of the old-fashioned palanquin type. On the way, they passed teahouses and shops, in which they saw people weaving silk tapestries on the handloom. There were two or three steep passes to be negotiated, boasting unrivalled scenery. There was also the alternative route by sea and yet another inland route, but assuredly the ride along the shore was the most thrilling experience.

Arriving at Atami, they took up quarters at the chief hotel, managed by Mr. Higuchi. He, his wife and his children could speak fluent English, though themselves Japanese. The hotel stood on a knoll in the centre of the town and so commanded a lovely panoramic view of the place. One might have said of it – 'It is English, quite English, you know', after the phrasing of a well-known London advertisement, and everything was in the best style both in respect of decoration and cooking. Atami was considered to be the best sanatorium in Japan. The famous Atami geyser was intermittently active and during the active period – that is, every 4 or 5 hours – it emitted its heating vapour. The health-giving stream, which ran down from the mountains above was conveyed to the hotel and could be enjoyed by application of the water or by the inhalation of the vapour that arose from it. Another remarkable feature of Atami was the Turkish bath, built on a plot of earth that generated the necessary heat without any artificial aid, and here one or two baths a day could be enjoyed with impunity.

As to the surrounding walks, they were delightful, and in the depths of the wood it was most refreshing to take tea in the little bungalows erected for that purpose, whilst on the hill-tops the scenery was ever beautiful and varied, with waterfalls tumbling amidst rocky crevasses and all around, the sweet smelling camphor trees, from which the natives constructed boxes, toys and trays, useful for keeping insects at bay. They also produced 'Gampi-ori', a fabric made of silk and cotton and mixed with a special kind of paper, known as 'Gapis'. On the beach there was bathing, and pleasure boats were provided for fishing in the bay. In short, there was plenty to do. The visitor's book revealed the popularity of the town, and whilst they were there, they had the amusement of meeting an Englishman from India, who was able to speak in pure Hindustani and whose flying visit they highly enjoyed. After a week's stay, they returned to Yokohama – this time by the easy route – and took the opportunity of visiting the Exhibition again, on a Japanese holiday.

It had been Dosebai's intention to visit the famous caves of Igoshi at Fujigama. She however, decided against the journey because of the steep climb but her sons went and thoroughly enjoyed it. Here an annual fair took place and the stalls were spread out in the shape of temples, these latter being built in the memory of certain saints. Inside the caves, the entrance to which was close to the sea and into which the sea waves roll, there were corridors of deities hewn out of

181

the rock, for Japan was a land of temples. It was hard to believe that the exquisite cave images were the work of human hands.

So, making many purchases in Yokohama and bidding a sweet goodbye to all their friends, the travellers made their way to the good ship 'Persia', lying far off in mid stream. Dosebai's packages, the result of too much shopping, had grown in bulk resulting in her last day or two in Yokohama to be fully occupied with packing. So whose fault was that? They left the harbour bar amid the fondest farewells of those of their friends who accompanied them to the 'Persia' with gifts of lovely flowers. Thus they left evergreen Japan and all its scenic wonders.

CHAPTER 26

ONWARDS TO THE UNITED STATES OF AMERICA
FROM SAN FRANCISCO TO NEW YORK OVERLAND

Nine sea days on the Pacific later, they reached Honolulu on the volcanic island of Oahu in Hawaii. On board were many American ladies and gentlemen who, like Dosebai and her sons, were globetrotting and with whom they had voyaged on the way to Japan. At Honolulu, there was time to pay a flying visit to the town and its environs. They gazed upon the thousands of coconut trees, the stately palms and cacti of the island and relished its clear air. Honolulu was a town of quite American proportions and magnificence with many fine buildings and a striking bronze statute of King Kamehameha. Perhaps the chief attraction of the place was the Aquarium, and it certainly had the most brilliant collection of multi-coloured fishes. The Aquarium was considered, by no less an authority than Dr. David Jordan of Stanford University, to be second to none in interest and importance.

The Bishop Museum was also very educational revealing as it did, the early life of the Hawaiians in their jungles, on the mountaintops and attired in their native dress – not to mention the brilliantly coloured feathers of now extinct birds woven into crowns with jewels and armouries displayed in glass cases. On leaving the guests were garlanded with *leis*, pretty garlands of sweet scented flowers and vines, which was a lovely custom. Taking a farewell look at Hawaii's lush tropical growth, its coconut trees, bananas, avocados and pineapples and all sorts of tropical fruit, they stood on deck and watched Honolulu gradually fade from view as they weighed anchor for San Francisco.

Amongst their fellow passengers was Mr. Frederic Dumont Smith of Kingsley, who represented Kansas in the American Congress. After a voyage of seventeen days, they reached San Francisco on August 23rd 1907 and entered the historic Golden Gate of California. During the voyage from Honolulu to San Francisco, Dosebai was snapshotted in her Indian dress by some gentlemen of the American Press, who turned out to be surprisingly knowledgeable about the Parsi faith, religion and social life. On landing, their belongings were searched and to tell the truth, the officials were not a little puzzled by her sari costume, wondering from whence they hailed, till a couple of ladies came forward and explained the peculiarities of Parsi and Indian dress. At length, they reached their hotel (Jefferson's) without paying a cent to the customs and settled down in all the comfort and luxury of a modern palace. As she shrewdly suspected, the reporter on board had improved the occasion as she found her picture and a graphic account of herself in the newspapers – a circumstance that naturally drew upon herself and her sons much attention.

San Francisco had suffered a terrible earthquake on April 18th 1906 and a mention may not be out of place. Traces of it were still visible and the catastrophe, like Death the Leveller, was no respecter of persons. Dosebai saw the city in the aftermath of this great disaster. It was noteworthy that the older houses seem to have withstood the shock relatively unharmed. Fire however, had been far more destructive than the earthquake itself, and there was widespread damage but it was comforting to think of the noble qualities of courage and self-sacrifice that became evident evoked by the widespread suffering and distress. Great praise was due to the Army, Navy and City services for the splendid work done by them in treating the injured and arresting the march of the flames. Just imagine devastation spread over twelve square miles and yet, as if by some magic wand, a new and more splendid San Francisco was rising up from the ruins, like a phoenix from the ashes! The city was once more being acclaimed as the Queen of America's Pacific seaboard. Of course, like all American cities, the buildings were enormously high, but they were characteristic of the 'big' style of doing things in the States. It was a constant surprise to Dosebai, this bigness of things.

Here, Sunday was observed as a general holiday and picnics were the order of the day, with children all around in gay dresses and thousands of people enjoying the lovely parks. Dosebai had already secured tickets for the resumption of their journey – this time by rail – and planned to spend the remaining days of their stay in seeing as much as they could of this amazing city. That Sunday they took a long drive through the Sutro and Golden Gate Parks where they saw amongst other sights, the statues of past Presidents. In the afternoon, they had a surprise visit from the only Parsi in San Francisco (yup, there was one there, too), Mr. Pestonjee Framjee Davar, of Messrs. Lombard and Scott Ltd. He told them about his recent sufferings and losses through earthquake and the subsequent fire. Yet, with that energy and enterprise so characteristic of the race, he had once more revived his fortunes, and this in a really short space of time.

The same evening, they drove to the famous Ocean Beach, above which, standing on a cliff at its very edge was Cliff House, presenting a solid square to all the winds that blow yet looking, in spite of all its wild weather experiences, as fresh as if it had been built yesterday. Close by were the Seal Rocks like giant needles, the haunt of sea lions, hundreds of which were often to be seen disporting themselves. Further up this hill, they came to the world-famous Sutro Baths (named after the donor) with five hundred bathing rooms, an amphitheatre capable of seating four thousand people and a promenade of the same capacity. (The Sutro Baths was a large, privately owned public saltwater swimming pool complex in the Lands End area of western San Francisco. It was built in 1896, and was located near the Cliff House, Seal Rocks and Sutro Heights Park. This incredible and very grand facility burned down in June 1966 and is now in ruins). The approach to the Sutro Baths was a long descent by way of a Grand Museum and a stage for spectators, and the distance from San Francisco was seven miles along a beautiful stretch of road. On their way, they saw the New Tavimont Hotel on the summit of Nol Hill – a palace of palaces – and the abode of merchant princes, surrounded by lovely orchards and playgrounds.

On Dosebai's return that night she enjoyed the company of several ladies interested in her dress, religion and educational systems but in the midst of it all, they were destined to witness a great fire – a gruesome reminder of those which created such devastation after the earthquake. It was a dreadful sight but was got under control in a wonderfully short time, though not before an appalling amount of destruction had been wrought. The very word 'fire' was enough to rouse the whole city and hundreds and thousands flocked to witness the conflagration and assist, where they could, the Fire Brigade. As for themselves, they were able, after such a spectacle, to more fully realize the horrors of April 1906.

San Francisco was built on hills and from heights approaching a thousand feet one could look down upon a magnificent vista of docks, streets, edifices, and beyond, the open sea. Not even Rome, Malta or Hong Kong could boast of such a view as that which the 'Queen of the Pacific' afforded. Their friend Mr. Davar offered to take them for a drive to the University of California, situated across the Bay at Berkeley; but owing to the exigencies of travel and lack of time at their disposal, they had to forego that pleasure and turn their thoughts to preparations for the long journey on the morrow. It was a great convenience that one's heavy packages and luggage could be booked right through and that however often one broke journey, they would be waiting for you at the other end. This was a distinct comfort to the globetrotter as was also the provision made for living and sleeping on board the express train.

Crossing by the Ferry they reached Oakland Pier Station on the opposite shore. Taking their seats in the very comfortable train, they were soon on their way to Chicago.

The first halt was Sacramento, where there was plenty of activity even though it was late at night and continuing their journey with the full moon shining in a cloudless sky, they enjoyed a mountain gradient climb. Truckee, the junction for the beautiful Lake Tahoe, was far behind them as they reached an altitude of seven thousand feet above sea level. There was then a long descent into spectacular scenery, with greenery all round and trees clinging to the mountainside.

On the third morning at 7 am, they reached Ogden, a major junction, from where they headed for Omaha, crossing nothing but mile upon mile of barren, monotonous country. It was a great relief, therefore, to reach lively Chicago on the fourth day after leaving San Francisco. What a busy place this lakeside city was, with its traffic and shipping! They had to cross the town in a special horse drawn omnibus to get the connection to New York. Everything – buildings, parks and vehicles, even the horses – was on a huge scale. Even the waiting rooms presented the appearance of large spacious halls.

The journey was resumed on the Michigan Central and Hudson River Railway – the Niagara Falls route – towards Detroit. The next morning having, on the previous halt, undergone the customary examination before entering Canada they arrived at the famous Falls. Here the train stopped for half an hour on the Canadian side at what was called Fall's View, where the vision of the stupendous cataract burst into view with the curve of the gigantic Horseshoe Fall magnificently conspicuous, as well as the river shining resplendent in the sun, sweeping onwards to its fall, and the Rapids below raging and roaring to their rest in the lake further down.

In Dosebai's own eloquent words, 'To realise the full effect of the Niagara Falls, you must see them from below. You must look upwards at the infinite grandeur that confronts you and must be in the midst, as it were, of the roar as the waters descend, whilst the mist blows in gusts about your head. As you look up at the vast tumbling mass of foam edged water, with the sounds of the world all lost in the mighty tumult of Nature, your whole being is filled with wonder and awe. Impressively beautiful too, are the views of the Falls from above, for then you see the sweep and grandeur of breadth of the great cataract such as you can never see from below. Yet, equally above as below are the Rapids – smooth, swift, shining above and seething below in a huge whirlpool! Indeed, a marvellous sight never ever to be forgotten'.

From Niagara Falls the journey continued on to Buffalo, down the Mohaw River Valley. The scenery was hugely varied. Now cities flashed into sight and now it was a quiet, green landscape reminiscent of England. At length, they reached Albany on the Hudson River and crossing the 'Hudson Highlands' (the Catskill Mountains region), they passed along the banks of the ever-widening river till, at its mouth – called the Yappanzee - stood New York City, the largest in the New World – the Metropolis of the Western Hemisphere – with its four million inhabitants, its wonderful buildings and famous streets and avenues.

It was in the evening of September 1st, after five days and five nights of continuous travel, that Dosebai and her sons reached America's commercial capital, and the sight of it was indeed, impressive. On settling down in their hotel, the next thought was of meeting their Parsi friends. They had been informed previously in Bombay, that several Parsi firms had been established in New York, including that of Mr. J.N. Tata. His sister, Mrs. Saklatwalla had also taken up residence here with her son. She was an old friend of Dosebai's and invited her to her home.

They walked down Broadway, full of theatres, huge offices and shops. They visited Wall Street, and in this part of the city were the tallest skyscrapers, that of Singer's having no less than forty-seven floors. (This building at 149 Broadway was the tallest construction at the time). There was the City Hall, the '*World*' and '*Tribune*' offices, New Trinity buildings and last but not least, the Customs House Building, with its statues ranged in front. In short, New York was a city of big streets, big buildings and big restaurants – the last named fell into two categories – those for the rich and those for the poor. Most Americans ate in restaurants and Dosebai noticed with interest that, whilst girls and women served at the poor people's restaurants (whatever they were), only men served as waiters and sommeliers in the grander establishments for the well-to-do classes. During their stay in New York they noticed how sympathetic with all things

Indian the American people really were. They had given practical proof of this by the establishment of charitable institutions under American Missions in different parts of India. Also, the Americans at the hotel enjoyed discussing India with them.

Soon after their arrival, they went to see Mrs. Saklatwalla, (née Tata) who lived in Riverside Avenue, one of the best locations in the city some ten miles away from the centre. From this part, there was a grand view of the Hudson River. They found their friend living alone, and were mutually very glad to spend a few hours together. Dosebai was struck by her friend's courage in leaving her own country and living in the midst of strangers all by herself. Of course, she had several maids and staff, but even so. On leaving her they returned by the subway (underground). On the way home, they visited William Whiteley's of New York (the original Whiteley's store was opened in Bayswater, London in 1863), her Parsi dress being the object of much curiosity and attention. Hundreds and thousands of people were always rushing about in New York and the citizens kept very late hours, a fact that doubtless, according to Dosebai, accounted for their shortened lives. The day after their arrival in New York, the inevitable reporter turned up and they had to undergo a volley of questions as to their nationality, religion, and the purpose of their long tour and also their opinion on the people and places they had seen. The conversation frequently turned to the question of their visiting Boston, Washington and other cities of America.

Dosebai was also advised to seek an interview with President Roosevelt, the much-loved and deservedly popular head of the American Republic.

The following morning Mr. Nusserwanjee Panthakee, now a naturalised American citizen, kindly took them for a ride in a 'sight-seeing car'. The tour was around Upper New York and included views of palatial residences of American millionaires, the Boulevards of Central Park, the Manhattan Viaduct with its unrivalled view of the Hudson River, the picturesque palisades of the Columbia University building, Public Libraries, monuments and statues, including those of Columbus and Washington, cathedrals, churches, hospitals, clubs and finally the tomb of General Grant, where they stopped for a few minutes. In Central Park there were many features of interest, including the Metropolitan museum of Art and Cleopatra's Needle, a fine structure of Egyptian antiquity, the pair to which was in London. Indeed, they had quite a surfeit of sightseeing, buildings and nothing but buildings being the prominent feature of the round.

The next morning Dosebai booked their passage in the '*Celtic*' for Liverpool. The vessel belonged to the White Star Line, and had a tonnage greater than that of any other of the Company's ships. She was due to sail on September 19th. Their friends persuaded them to remain longer and visit Washington and the Jamestown Exhibition before leaving America, so they changed their bookings from the '*Celtic*' to the '*St. Paul*' of the American Line bound for Southampton on the 28th of September, thereby giving them a full week longer.

The next tour was around Lower New York, and this time the Brooklyn Bridge over the East River was the objective. Completed in 1883 it was a 7,000 ft long suspension bridge, the centre span being 1,600 ft, height from the water 1,135 ft and width 118 ft. Six lines of railway traversed this bridge, besides roadways and footways. All things considered, it was a remarkable monument of engineering skill. On their return to Manhattan from the Brooklyn side of the river, they drove through the streets lit up by thousands of powerful electric lamps. This was a city that would never know the natural darkness of a city asleep.

CHAPTER 27

WASHINGTON AND THE JAMESTOWN EXHIBITION AND TO ENGLAND ONCE MORE

At the crack of dawn they set off by the Pennsylvanian Railway for Washington and the Jamestown Exhibition. The route was via ferryboat across the Hudson to Jersey City and then by rail to the political capital of the States, Washington D.C. They passed Philadelphia, the capital of Pennsylvania, and then Baltimore and at length reached Washington, putting up at the Burton Hotel. Apparently, this spacious edifice was built in 1780 by General Washington himself and was situated at 226, North Capitol Street and located delightfully on Capitol Hill. Directly opposite were the Capitol and the Library. Washington was the tidiest and cleanest city Dosebai had ever seen, with its broad streets and well-planned avenues. It was quite a hero-worshipping city with memorials and statues everywhere.

A pyramidal superstructure of aluminium surmounted the Washington Monument, which was 555 feet high. The Monument was opened to the public on 9th October 1888, although construction started much earlier with the cornerstone being laid on the 4th of July 1848. Thousands attended the ceremony, including a relatively unknown Congressman named Abraham Lincoln. Inside were many memorial stones, and the interior was lit throughout with electricity. (Electricity was still quite novel for Dosebai). The total cost was 1,300,000 dollars and it was at that time, the highest work of masonry in the world. (As the tallest man-made structure, the Eiffel Tower superseded it in 1889).

The White House itself was a construction of grandeur and beauty. George Washington laid the corner stone of this building in

1792 and lived to see it completed. In the company of his wife, Martha, he walked through all the rooms just a few days before his death in 1799. Close to the White House was the National Library or Library of Congress, erected at a cost of 6,000,000 dollars and admittedly one of the most beautiful buildings in the world – a product of everything that was aesthetic in architecture and art and in point of fact, America's high-watermark of architectural achievement. All the architects, painters and sculptors were Americans, and they must have had a great sense of pride in achieving this. Americans, of course, were already of immigrant stock from the cultured lands of Europe and the rest of the world and had brought a rich assortment of artistic talent with them.

The hill on which the Capitol was situated commanded a fine view of the River Potomac, flowing majestically in the valley below. The crowning glory of the Capitol was its imposing dome of fluted Corinthian columns above the central building, terminating in a lantern surmounted by the Statue of Freedom, 300 feet above the Esplanade. The dome was made of iron and so constructed as to expand and contract 'like the folding and unfolding of a lily' with the variations of temperature. The view from the dome, reached by a winding staircase, was superb and amply repaid the tiring ascent. On entering the Capitol, the National Statuary Hall, semi-circular in shape, first claimed Dosebai's attention.

The Hall of Representatives, located in the South Wing of the Capitol was a legislative chamber of unparalleled beauty and splendour. The Supreme Court Room and many other rooms in the building were of uniform beauty and elegance and it was impossible to single out any particular room for special mention.

During Dosebai's stay in America, one of her favourite visits was to Norfolk to see the Jamestown Exhibition – or Exposition, as they called it. They travelled by the night steamer, reaching their destination the next morning. After refreshing themselves, they went by motorcar to the Exhibition – a cheap ride there and back for a dollar. Jamestown had been a settlement since 1607 and here were planted, so to speak, the first seeds of the Republican Tree. The town was situated in the Province of Virginia and the Exhibition was being held in order to celebrate the tercentenary of permanent English settlement in America. All the States were represented in the exhibits, and there were military and naval drills, parades and manoeuvres. There were buildings that had been especially constructed to represent different styles of architecture from the many States, varying from the year 1607 to the year 1907. Held on the seashore and the first of its kind, it was a wonderful array of historical and industrial achievements, every conceivable branch of the arts and sciences being exemplified in the thousands of objects daily visible to the millions of visitors.

Now, would you believe it - at the Exhibition Dosebai found a stall belonging to a Parsi, displaying a really marvellous collection of ivories, tapestries, bronze and other oriental wares – the first from India to be displayed in a western exhibition. The crowning exhibit was a reproduction of the ancient and historical Jain Temples of Palitana – a wonderfully carved teakwood model, representing all the Gods of ancient India and the result of many years work by sixty-four renowned Indian artists. (Palitana in Gujerat, is the world's only mountain that has more than 900 temples on it and is the world's largest temple complex. It is a totally incredible sight to visit). Dosebai felt sincerely grateful for the health and vigour that enabled her to see, within the space of three months, two such superb exhibitions as the one at Tokyo and the other in the States. On leaving again for New York they caught a last farewell of shore and Exhibition, all beautifully lit up with electric light.

Sailing into New York harbour, the majestic Statue of Liberty and the great ships like floating palaces arrested their attention and the sight of New York reminded them once more of its busy life and immense wealth. The next day, Dosebai paid another visit to Mrs. Saklatwalla – a farewell visit to a dear friend. The time passed all too quickly, and almost before she realised the hour of departure had arrived, they had taken up their berths on the steamship 'St. Paul' for Plymouth and Southampton - a voyage of eight days. The weather was stormy for the greater part and calmed down only towards the close of the run and the majority of the passengers were seasick and had to keep to their cabins. However, on nearing England, they got up a concert. Reaching Plymouth, they stopped to land the Mails and disembark many passengers for the Continent. They then continued to Southampton, where they arrived at 8 p.m. and immediately caught the Express train to London.

Dosebai and her boys had been away from home for five months and varied had been their experiences. Arriving in London, the Bedford Hotel in Russell Square became their temporary home. Then, having met by lucky chance, some Parsi friends, (now there's a surprise), they found snug and suitable quarters in the vicinity of Gordon Square.

The next day she paid a visit to Mrs. Boyce, who lived in England with her children, for their education, at West Dulwich. It so happened about this time that Dosebai needed medical aid, as did also her sons, so they were advised to move to New Cross. In London, rooms could be engaged per day, week or month according to one's requirements, and so she was quite easily able to quit her Bloomsbury rooms for those at Jerningham Road, Telegraph Hill. A visit to the city the following day called Sir Owen Burne to mind, and to her great sorrow, Dosebai heard that he had recently lost his second wife. He himself was out of town, so they sent a letter of condolence. Strangely enough and sadly enough, too, Sir Owen Burne's first wife had died in 1878 just before Dosebai's arrival in England and now the sad occurrence of the loss of his second wife took place just prior to her third visit. In the kindest manner possible, Sir Owen wrote to them from his Hampshire address, assuring of his regret at his sudden and unavoidable absence from London through sad bereavement.

A very convenient feature of London life was the Accommodating Transit Agency, of which Carter Paterson & Co. was a typical example. One placed the legend C.P. in one's window, and in a short time along came a van, and off went your luggage to its new destination. What a saving of time and money, too! While at New Cross, Dosebai received a letter from her dear friend Mrs.

Ahlers, announcing her return from the Isle of Wight and promising an early visit.

Lady Scott, wife of Sir J. Scott, late a High Court Judge in Bombay, sent her an invitation to a lecture on Indian Female Education, to be given under the auspices of the National Indian Association by Mr. N.G. Welinkar, formerly a Professor at the Wilson College, Bombay. Needless to say, she enjoyed it immensely for she had always been personally interested in promoting female education in India. Sir William Lee-Warner presided and amongst those present were Dr. Pollen, Sir Charles Lyall, Lady Scott and many other Anglo-Indian ladies and gentlemen. Mr. Welinkar, the lecturer, had founded a Poor Boys' Seminary in Bombay, named after India's Grand Old Man, Mr. Dadabhoy Naoroji, which was built on a plot of ground owned by Dosebai and so had endeared himself to the Parsi community and Dosebai was especially touched to hear him refer to her mother (Meheribai) as the first Indian lady to send her daughter to the English Seminary in Bombay.

As the winter days closed in, her eldest son was taken ill and for a time his state of health was so critical that she had to call in Sir Douglas Powell M.D., Physician to the King but after long, careful nursing her son recovered and she was able to prolong her stay in England.

It was now the depth of the English winter and Dosebai spent a good deal of her time visiting the London shops. The Secretary of the Society of Arts sent her a card of invitation to a lecture on the wild beasts of India and she was especially interested inasmuch as it was delivered by an old attorney friend of hers, Mr. Gilbert, of the firm of Payne and Gilbert. It also gave her the opportunity of meeting some Bombay friends.

After the New Year came the opening ceremony of Parliament on the 29th January 1908 and Dosebai had the privilege of a seat in the Royal gallery to witness it. She went in Parsi costume and was fortunate enough to occupy a seat in the front row, in the full gaze of Their Majesties, she being the only Parsi woman from India present.

Her dress drew upon her quite an unusual amount of attention and prompted the usual questions.

Their Majesties were announced with a bugle fanfare and entering the Throne Room with all pomp and circumstance befitting the occasion, they at once became the observed of the observers – the focus of one of the most brilliant functions it had been her lot to witness. As Their Majesties walked to their Thrones, Dosebai was near enough to be able to exchange greetings, and the same pleasing experience was hers on their leaving. After the ceremony, she returned home in a motorcar. The next day, she saw articles about her in several London papers, and friends who were interested in her doings sent her cuttings from the Press.

Whilst in England Dosebai became a motorist (she was only 77), and really found it to be a most convenient and expeditious means of getting about. She finally resolved to buy one, use it here and then have it shipped to Bombay. Two years earlier, in 1906, her grandson's wife, Tehmina (my grandmother) aged 20, had entered the Aga Khan Challenge motor race from Poona to Satara (in India) and had caused quite an uproar as she was the only female competitor, and of course, also won the race. She was awarded a beautifully engraved silver chalice, which is now in my possession. She was, more than likely, the first Indian Parsi woman to drive a car, so no doubt, her husband's grandmother was not going to be outdone.

On one of Dosebai's motor drives in London, they went to the Crystal Palace, in the vicinity of which at West Dulwich, lived her friend Mrs. Boyce. They also went to Sir. Robert West's house with her and spent a very pleasant evening meeting Mrs. Cooke, the wife of Surgeon-General Cooke and her daughter and Lady West, wife of the well-known Judge of the Bombay High Court. Dosebai met these ladies again after thirty-four years so it was therefore, a memorable event.

In the meantime, the Marquis of Ripon, whose sympathetic nature had been so well known and who was the most popular Viceroy

India had ever had, granted Dosebai an interview, and promised to use his influence in securing for her a presentation in person to Their Majesties the King and Queen. Lord Ripon was then 80, but he still retained much of his vigour unabated, even as when she had seen him many years ago at Government House parties in Bombay. Whilst waiting for the return of the King from his cruise in the Baltic, Dosebai attended the annual banquet of the Parsi community on the 21st March (*Jamshedi-Navroz*). On this occasion, Lord Ampthill, the Governor of Madras (and for a time Viceroy of India), next to whom she sat and Mr. H. Cox M.P. were amongst the distinguished visitors.

On the following Sunday, when she went to Mr. D.P. Cama's place, she met the young son of her late cousin Mrs. K. R. Cama, who had recently married an English girl. Dosebai noticed with pleasure, too, that the Cama family were carrying on business very successfully. The Camas were the first Parsis to establish business offices in London. Dosebai also met Sir M.M. Bhownagree, a gentleman who had a distinguished career both in and out of Parliament and was a thoroughly representative and public-spirited member of the community. He had been settled in England for more than twenty years and for ten years had served India, in the House of Commons, with zeal and marked ability. Her visit to his house was one of her red-letter events.

They conversed on quite a variety of topics, and he invited her to an 'At Home' of the National Indian Association in the Jehangir Hall at the Imperial Institute. The hall itself had been a gift from Dosebai's own cousin, and such perpetuity of the Parsi name and prestige was extremely gratifying to her. With such a reference it seems most fitting to close this account of her wanderings with just a passing mention of her visit to the Queen's Hall, where she enjoyed the best of music, and a visit to the Caxton Hall, where a meeting, presided over by Sir W. Wedderburn, and addressed by Mr. Keir-Hardie and members of the forward school, gave ample evidence of the sympathy of so many notable Englishmen with the Indian Empire and all that made for its true progress.

Something that pleased Dosebai a lot was that, in this advanced age, women were being encouraged to leave their homes and travel far and wide. She received an invitation to a Tea Party from her old friend, Mrs. Ezra, at Berkley Square, Piccadilly. It was no small pleasure to see her friend settled in London with her grown-up daughters and sons, who were all very young when Dosebai had seen them last in Calcutta. Dosebai was living very far from town and from most of her friends who were permanent residents here, but her motorcar made visiting so easy that she never felt lonely as constant exchanges of visits took place between them. On the 7th May, she attended a gathering held at the Duke of Westminster's Grosvenor House near Hyde Park and found it most informative as she had the occasion to meet several foremost ladies of rank taking keen interest in the cause of women. The Suffragette movement in England was also gathering momentum at this time, which must have interested Dosebai considerably.

A few days after this, there was a *Tableau Vivant* held at Caxton Hall, in aid of the India Famine Fund to which a large number of Indian ladies and gentlemen went in their own national dress, which was a unique sight in London in those days. She also met another old friend, Mrs. Vakil, who had travelled to London from Bombay all alone, on account of her son's illness. Dosebai was delighted to note that, only a few years ago, ladies of her community would never have moved about so boldly and freely as they did now. Not only had the ideas of orthodox men changed, but also those of women. When, in the eighteen-sixties and seventies her own daughter used to travel between Bombay and London all alone, what a great outcry was raised by the fathers and grandfathers of the same families whose younger generations were now following the example. The credit for this emancipated attitude was due to none other than her old and revered mother, Bai Meheribai, who had suffered so much at the hands of bigoted orthodoxy.

At long last, spring arrived and with it, the Franco-British Exhibition, was opened in London on May 14th 1908 with due pomp and ceremony.

198

As she lived very far from town and Shepherd's Bush where the Exhibition was being held, as well as far away from many of her friends, she resolved to change residence. She chose a house at Cambridge Garden, Notting Hill, which was close to the residence of Mr and Mrs D.P. Cama, as well as to the Exhibition ground. Every day there was a different programme of events at the Exhibition. The Olympic Games also took place in White City that year at around the same time. This was part of the *entente-cordiale*, so with the help of the Franco-British Exhibition Association, the Stadium in London was constructed in the short space of two years. Incidentally, it was the only Olympics when Britain came out on top of the Medals table.

In the first week of the Exhibition, she went to see the Bazaar, in aid of the Zenana Mission School, opened by H.R.H. Princess Christian, held at Morley Hall in Hanover Square, where a great many Royals were also present. Three days after this, President Armand Fallieres of France made a special trip to London. There was a public reception and it was a truly grand sight to see his progress from the railway station to the French Embassy. The people of England received him with great enthusiasm.

The next day when he, in company with the King, entered the Exhibition ground, it was so densely crowded that for a time it was difficult to move from one section to another. The spectacle was a grand one. There was a public ovation, fully manifested in the *entente cordiale* existing between the two great nations. Dosebai never found a day's rest, kind friends constantly inviting her to one gathering or another. She attended some of the Olympic Games and went to the opening, by the Countess of Lytton, of the Southwark and Lambeth Exhibition of paintings at the Borough Polytechnic Institute. Here, Dosebai had the opportunity of making the acquaintance of the Ex-Vicerine's good-natured daughter-in-law, from whom she heard that the Dowager Countess was on the Continent and not likely to return soon to London.

Every day brought with it some new amusement and she did not fail to visit the Hungarian Exhibition at Earl's Court in the company of her friend, Mrs D.P. Cama. Although it was on a very small scale, they still found it worth experiencing, and passed the day in the merry company of many Parsi friends who were also there.

In the midst of this imperial city, something that surprised Dosebai considerably was the purchase of York House in Twickenham by Mr R. J. Tata, who was living in London with his wife. It was originally a royal palace. Dosebai, along with two lady friends, was invited to tea, so they had the opportunity of seeing an old royal house occupied by her Parsi friends. What astonished her most was the decoration of the Hall with Indian black wood carved furniture, in which were some of the settees and tables which had originally belonged to her in Bombay and now occupied a place in this royal house. She was tickled pink! Mr and Mrs Tata showed them great hospitality. Although the drive to Twickenham was a long and tedious one, they found it a very enjoyable occasion. It was no small pleasure to find young descendants of old orthodox families enjoying life so well and free from all the old world prejudices of their forefathers.

As the day for the Presentation to Their Majesties was drawing near, Dosebai was very busy with her dress for the occasion. Sir Curzon Wyllie, Political A.D.C. to the Secretary of State for India had arranged everything. Dosebai, in company with her son, was invited to the India Office, where Sir Wyllie received them and explained everything about the arrangements for her reception at Windsor instead of Buckingham Palace. Dosebai was pleased about this, as a Garden Party at Windsor would be a most colourful, grand and socially satisfying event to attend.

CHAPTER 28

BEING PRESENTED TO THEIR MAJESTIES AT WINDSOR 1908

Dosebai now set about preparing for the most exciting and interesting event of her tour. To be presented to the Sovereign and the Queen had been the most ardent wish of her life, and in the evening of her career, it was about to be fulfilled.

Buckingham Palace and Windsor Castle formed the theatre of the most imposing ceremonies and functions. The British certainly knew how to put on a good show. In the early twentieth century, Court ceremonies were more approachable, full of life and great formalities, sufficiently imposing to give them the necessary seriousness but with slightly less of the stiffness that had characterised the Court ceremonials of past monarchs of Great Britain. Dosebai felt that no one who had witnessed them could deny that they were worthy, in their splendour, of the greatest Empire the modern world had ever seen.

When Court functions and presentations were in the air, the close observer was aware of an indefinable something in the atmosphere. There was a palpable stir among the great of the land when the King and Queen came to town with their retinue. The invitations were issued two or three weeks ahead and many were the manoeuvres that were resorted to for securing admission into the charmed circle of Their Majesties' guests. Dosebai had already set on foot the machinery for her presentation and it was her great, good fortune that kind and influential friends arranged everything for her. She would always be grateful for this.

To commemorate this wonderful event with something worthy of the occasion, she had long contemplated presenting to Their Majesties the King Emperor Edward VII and Queen Alexandra a precious and beautiful gift. She had been busily working on a cap and dress trimmings, which she was ambitious enough to hope would be accepted by Their Majesties. The cap was of black velvet, decorated with enamelled miniature portraits of Queen Victoria, the Prince Consort, the King-Emperor Edward VII, Queen Alexandra and other members of the Royal Family. Between the paintings, was pure gold thread embroidery of intricate design and a Crown, studded with rubies and diamonds, surmounted the miniature of the King.

The heavily embroidered dress front and bands were of exquisite design, there were stars and flowers interlaced with gold and silver thread and studded with pearls. The effect was very striking and was sure to appeal to Her Majesty's love of precious stones and embroidered work. A suitable box of carved sandalwood had been prepared for these articles, and contained two portaits of Dosebai, one taken nearly 30 years ago and another during her present sojourn in London. The casket bore the following inscription:

'To His Majesty the King-Emperor Edward VII and
Her Majesty Queen-Empress Alexandra,
The embroidered work of Their Majesties'
Loyal and Faithful Subject
Dosebai Cowasji Jessawalla'

She was often asked who had designed the work. It went against the grain to have to answer repeatedly that both the design and the execution were entirely her own. Indeed, designing pretty things was a hobby of hers and she had not only, very often, prepared her own dress materials but had done much designing work for others. A piece of her embroidery had been exhibited in London in 1886 at the Indian and Colonial Exhibition and was awarded a Gold Medal.

It was her long cherished dream that the articles should be tendered to Their Majesties with her own hands. That they would be accepted by them, with as much graciousness as they actually did, was beyond her wildest dreams. Presentation at Court was always a matter of no small difficulty and one involving many formalities. To be presented to one's Sovereign was a hallmark of social status and respectability and everyone was anxious to secure the honour. Permission was always necessary and in the present case it was not only readily granted but special features were introduced in it.

Early in January, when His Majesty opened the Houses of Parliament, Dosebai happened to be one of the privileged spectators amongst the bejewelled peeresses in the Lords. The late Marquis of Ripon had very kindly interested himself in her behalf and had procured her a seat in the Peeress's Gallery. Here in the midst of a galaxy of everything that was brilliant, she had the satisfaction of knowing that she was the cynosure of all beholders. Her dress, which was a Parsi costume in keeping with her age, was suitable to the occasion and the august assembly, the opening of which she witnessed.

This appearance in Parliament in the Peeress's gallery of Parliament paved the way to the Presentation. Shortly after the opening ceremony of Parliament, she had an interview with Lord Ripon. In the course of the conversation, he remarked that it would not be in the fitness of things that she should go away from England without having had an audience of Their Majesties, and with his ready kindness, promised to arrange the matter for her. The Honourable Lady Knollys (Lady in Waiting to the Queen) was requested to sound the Queen's wishes on the subject. Lord Ripon also asked his son (then Earl de Grey) Treasurer of the Queen's Household, to interest himself in the matter, which he did. As Dosebai hailed from India, it was thought necessary, as a matter of formality, to communicate with the India Office and Lord Morley was written to.

Another friend, Sir Owen Tudor Burne, was also equally kind and helpful in the matter. He fully approved of the idea of her presentation and promised to speak to Lady Knollys and Lord Morley about it. The matter was also mentioned to Sir William Curzon Wyllie, who was also very sympathetic and promised to do all he could to further her wishes. It is sad to reflect that, by the time Dosebai published her memoirs, all three gentlemen who kindly helped her on this matter were no more. She was particularly shocked when an Indian assassinated Sir Curzon Wyllie. Her heart went out to poor Lady Curzon Wyllie in her irreparable bereavement. Dosebai hoped that these cruel and heart-rending episodes would prove but fleeting shadows, and that the atmosphere of the future would never be clouded by such calamities. It is just as well that she did not live long enough to see India gain Independence!

It was at first, under contemplation that she should be received, by Their Majesties, at Buckingham Palace. It was very thoughtful of the Royal hosts to think of saving her the journey to Windsor, and was indicative of the unvarying courtesy and consideration that the gracious Sovereign and his Consort showed in their dealings with all subjects, of high or low degree, with people of all nationalities and all countries. But, as a Garden Party was to be held at Windsor on the 20th June, a date not far distant, Dosebai desired that the presentation should take place at that function, as it would at the same time, give her an opportunity of witnessing a pleasant function and meeting many friends. At the instance of Sir Curzon Wyllie, the articles that were to be presented to Their Majesties were forwarded a day ahead to Windsor to save her the trouble of carrying them with her.

The cap and the dress materials were duly placed before Their Majesties, who were graciously pleased to accept them and expressed their thanks at the interview, which followed the next day. Dosibai's elder son, Dadabhoy, was once again attacked with fever and confined to his room, so she left for Windsor in her trusty motorcar, accompanied by her younger son, Jamsetjee. But they were not destined to reach the castle without mishaps. They were about three miles from Windsor, when a tyre burst and they had to stop to repair the damage. Whilst they were thus detained, many distinguished guests proceeding to the party passed them, several of whom very kindly offered to help. But as they expected to be on their way again very soon they thankfully declined the kind offers. Tyre troubles, Dosebai decided, were the down side of motoring and their penalty that afternoon was being three quarters of an hour late for the Royal party.

The day opened fine and sunny, but in the course of the afternoon, dark clouds rolled in ominously, suggestive of a thunderstorm. Happily however, the clouds dispersed and delightful sunshine followed. The sun's rays were considerably modified by a cool north wind, which blew out the Royal Standard from its flagstaff on the Round Tower, and made the crowd come out from the shade into the sunshine. With such ideal weather conditions it was no wonder that there was a large attendance at the party and that the guests numbered between eight and nine thousand. Long in advance, a crowd of expectant onlookers was gathered outside the Palace. They swarmed around all the approaches, peering eagerly into every carriage as each one came rolling up. The decorative guard of honour on duty at the entrance gave the necessary spit and polish military touch to the portals of the Castle.

As they approached the Castle throngs of people who were collected on either side of the road, made different surmises regarding the two of them. Some exclaimed: 'Here goes an Indian Princess and her kinsman', others called them 'great people from Armenia.' They were highly amused at some of the comments.

Their late arrival due to the motor mishaps caused her no little trepidation as to their reception. But happily, everything passed off smoothly. On reaching the entrance and showing their cards, a dignified and stiff-looking officer helped her to alight from the car and escorted them a short distance to the main part of the gathering. The delay in their arrival, it seemed, had caused some dislocation in the programme and Sir William Curzon-Wyllie and the other officials responsible for the management were casting anxious glances in the direction of the entrance for their arrival. They were, however, too well bred to let it show either by word or sign. As soon as they had come up and before they had time to tender apologies for the delay, they were hurried straight to the Royal Tents, across the Great Lawn. The scene that unfolded itself when they had time to look about them was very grand and imposing. All the elite of London were there, making a great display of dress and jewellery and the scene was one that defied description.

Long before Dosebai's arrival, the King and Queen and members of the Royal Family had arrived on the Lawn, where they remained for nearly two hours. The King wore a blue frock coat and white top hat, a red tie and a flower in the buttonhole. The Queen was wearing a costume in her favourite shade of mauve with a toque to match, adorned with flowers of the same shade. The dress was of pale orchid *ninon-de soie,* charmingly embroidered. The bodice was finished with white tulle and in the light neck-ruffle, gleamed beautiful diamonds and pearls.

They had been too late to witness the arrival of the King and Queen, who had entered the Gardens from the Castle and found most of the guests already assembled.

Immediately upon Dosebai's arrival they were escorted to the Queen, who was in her spacious pavilion. She received them very graciously and looked sweet and smiling in her exquisite dress resplendent with jewellery. On their being presented, she shook hands with Dosebai and Jamsetjee and conversed with them with great interest for some time. She told Dosibai that she very much admired her hand-work and wondered at her zeal in embroidering with such detail at such an advanced age and when she learnt that it was always a pleasure for Dosibai to do needlework of every sort, in spite of the infirmities of old age, she was both pleased and impressed. Queen Alexandra also gave her credit for undertaking such a long and tedious journey at her age. Dosebai, fittingly, thanked Her Majesty for her kindness.

The most interesting part of the conversation was with reference to the Cap. Her Majesty thanked Dosibai profusely for having presented the King with an exquisite and unique Cap and her with such a beautiful Dress Front.

Duty bound, Dosibai expressed her gratitude for Her Majesty's graciousness in accepting the same. Her son had carried with him a box of flowers to be offered to Their Majesties. A magnificent garland of roses of the hue the Queen most liked was now put round her neck, and a bouquet of flowers presented to her. As Dosebai did this, she expressed her heartfelt wishes for the Queen's long life and prosperity and pronounced benedictions in true Parsi fashion. With this, the interview came to an end.

As they proceeded along the Lawns, His Majesty the King was seen coming towards them. As soon as he came near, Dosebai and her son were duly presented to his Majesty, who enthusiastically shook hands with them. He looked in splendid health and smiling all the time, conversed with them. They remained talking for about a quarter of an hour, during which Dosebai remarked that she had had the privilege of meeting him in Bombay in 1875 when he visited India. He looked pleased, and observed that it was many years ago, when he was quite a young man. She further assured him that the Parsis were very happy under his benign rule, at which he expressed satisfaction. He also gave her great credit for courage and energy in undertaking a voyage round the world at her time of life and thanked her appreciatively for the hand embroidered cap that she had personally made for him. Bowing her thanks, she asked permission to present him with the bouquet and garland of roses, to which, he kindly consented. A benediction similar to that in the case of the Queen was pronounced, and His Majesty went on his way, leaving them charmed with his affability.

Lady Curzon Wyllie then led them to one of the four refreshment tents, where bowls of La France roses adorned the tables set with gold service and Sevres china. On either side of the exteriors of the tents were high groups of hydrangeas and spirea, ferns and exotic plants from the Royal gardens at Frogmore. Lady Wyllie offered them tea and looked after them exceedingly well. In the refreshment tent, they were introduced to a number of distinguished personages. From a copy of the Court Circular of the day, we now know that Sir Arthur Conan Doyle was one of the guests, along with Dr. Saint-Saens, the French composer. It makes interesting reading. Leaving the tent, they walked on to the Lawn, which was studded with Princes, Dukes, Chiefs, Marquises and other distinguished personages. Now and then as she passed along, some of them would graciously introduce themselves to her.

207

They spent some time in mixing with the guests and admiring the arrangements made for the afternoon. The gathering was a very large and brilliant one and thoroughly representative of British society. Not only were all the best known people of rank and fashion present, but the most eminent representatives of literature, art, drama and the church were there. India was well represented by several Princes and Chiefs, some of whom were accompanied by their ladies. No small part of the colourful and spectacular effect was due to the Indian and Japanese Princes, in their gold turbans and coats of many colours. Their picturesque embroidered dresses with the beautiful saris of their ladies, wrought in gold and silver enhanced the effect. Ambassadors, Ministers and Staffs of the Embassies and Legations represented the diplomatic circle. Particularly noticeable were the King's Indian Orderlies in their fine uniforms.

They remained at Windsor for more than two hours, talking to friends and meeting different people. Amongst those they met were well-known Bombay friends. They saw Sir Raymond West and Lady West, Sir John and Lady Jardine and many others. Their Highnesses the Nawab Saheb and Begum Saheb of Janjira were also there, the latter in a most bewitching Oriental costume. They were on their European Tour and were spending the season in London.

During the time that they spent at the party, they received more than one kind message from the Queen, enquiring how they were enjoying themselves. These were amongst the traits of kindness that endeared Queen Alexandra to her subjects.

At a quarter to seven, the National Anthem, played by the Band of the Grenadier Guards, was the signal for the departure of the Royal party, and the guests began to disperse.

Dosebai came away from the Royal Garden Party well pleased with their reception and filled with joy and pleasure at all that they had seen, and the great kindness that they had experienced. An additional honour awaited them. Their motor having been disabled, they were very courteously offered a royal carriage to take them to Windsor Station. Thus was seen the curious spectacle of an septuagenarian Parsi Lady and her son, driving in an equipage having the royal red colour and bearing the Royal Crest, much to the surprise of the onlookers.

The London Press, in describing the garden party made a very touching mention of her presentation and of the beautiful gifts that Their Majesties were pleased to accept from her.

Hand embroidered and jewelled Cap for King Edward VII and
Dress Front for Queen Alexandra in gold and silver thread with
pearls.

Detail of Cap with miniatures of the Royal Family
surrounded by precious stones.

Interior of the Casket

CHAPTER 29

RETURN TO INDIA

As Dosebai's departure from England was drawing near, many of her old and respected friends invited them to tea or 'At Home' parties. Amongst these friends was Sir George Birdwood, who had such a high regard for the Parsi community that he had not forgotten them, although it was a long time since he returned from India. He lived at Ealing and for the pleasure of meeting Lady Birdwood and other members of the family, Dosebai happily accepted an invitation to visit them. Sir George was delighted to see them. He expressed his appreciation in a letter to her and about a week before she left London, he came to bid her adieu and showered on her all manner of good wishes for her future happiness. It was indeed a happy meeting for both of them, as he was also on the verge of 77. On her return from Ealing, she received another interesting invitation from Sir John and Lady Jardine, to meet them at St. Stephen's Hall, Westminster.

Sir John Jardine was once a very popular Judge of the Bombay High Court, and Lady Jardine, too, was a popular personage, taking a keen interest in the cause of Indian women. It was a congenial and productive meeting and a pleasant evening was passed in their company reminiscing of the past.

Her old friend, Mr. D.P.Cama had a birthday around this time. As a true Zoroastrian, he charitably distributed a substantial sum amongst the poorer classes every year. Although he had been living in London for the past forty years, he had not forgotten this old Parsi tradition. It was good for Dosebai to see a member of her community giving money to charities, without distinction of caste or creed. During the last few days of her stay, almost all her Parsi friends as well as many of her old and new English acquaintances came to bid her goodbye. Sir Owen Burne, too, came down from his country seat and paid his last and memorable visit only two days before her departure. This was a last visit because, soon after her return to Bombay, he died after a short illness.

As she found her motorcar very handy and cheap in the end, she kept it till the last days of her stay in London and as she had resolved to take it to Bombay, she had it packed and despatched to Bombay by a tramp boat going direct to Bombay, through Messrs. Thomas Cook and Son. (How on earth do you pack a motorcar)? The price she paid for the freight was very high, but the consolation she had was that it arrived safely at the exact time she arrived in Bombay. As the commission was entrusted to Thomas Cook and Son, they had every facility, as to the payment of freight, duty and clearing from the dock in Bombay on delivery. As it was undoubtedly a luxury to drive a motorcar in the city of London and its environments, she felt its absence much for a week or so. Then, once more, the old tramp with horse and carriage was renewed.

The Royal Garden Party brought her stay in London to an end and they arranged to sail back to Bombay direct by sea instead of taking an overland route, but for more than a fortnight they could not get passages as no cabins were available and it looked as if they would have to postpone their departure, when Sir Owen Burne came to their rescue. As Director of the P & O Company, (there is nothing like knowing the right people), he had much influence, and a word from him caused all difficulties to vanish and at last, they succeeded in securing their passage by an Australian mail-boat, *the S.S.Victoria* sailing on 31st July from Tilbury Docks, London, transferring at Aden onto the *S.S.Caledonia* for Bombay. As they were sailing from Tilbury Dock, all their heavy luggage had to be despatched at least forty-eight hours before the sailing of the vessel. The arrangement was so efficient that not one article was misplaced, notwithstanding such heavy passenger traffic. One was cautioned to label and number each and every package or bundle of article with one's name and destination, so that nothing could be misdirected or lost during the voyage. As for collection and shipment of baggage, one informed the Company seventy-two hours before the sailing, and the London Parcels Delivery Company sent their cart and men to collect the baggage and convey it to be shipped on board, saving all the trouble of dragging one's luggage along personally.

Hearing of Dosebai's imminent return to India, the Editor of the *Indian Magazine and Review,* Miss A.A. Smith, came to see her, and had a long interview with her.

The temptation to live in London never abated, and on the evening of her last day she attended an 'At Home' in her honour, at Mrs. Smith's, where she saw Indian and English friends mixing freely. Here, everyone was surprised to hear that she was to leave London the next morning. They were there till late, enjoying themselves heartily and she was delighted to observe the friendliness that existed between the different communities.

It was a happy morning on the 31st July when they all got ready to start on their return voyage. Her friends arrived with bouquets of flowers. With their best wishes for a bon voyage they left their temporary home at Cambridge Gardens and went to Liverpool Street Station to go to Tilbury Dock. Here, she met Mrs. D.P.Cama with her friends, who had come with flowers and garlands to see them off. Once they were on board the *S.S.Victoria* they saw Mr. Courtney of the London office, who left a good word for them with the ship's officers. The P&O officials, from Captain Haddock to the Pursers, were kind to them and placed them in spacious cabins, treating them with great distinction on the voyage. There was great excitement amongst the lively company of young and elderly passengers around them and just after 2 o'clock, the *S.S. Victoria* steamed out, homeward bound.

They settled in comfortably and had a very pleasant voyage to Gibraltar, where they arrived on the 4th August. The night before, there was a grand concert presented by some of the passengers. At Gibraltar, a great number left the ship as many of them were students from different universities going to enjoy their holidays. From here, after a halt of some six hours, they proceeded towards Marseilles arriving two days later. The steamship anchored for the night as it had to pick up passengers coming overland from London. During the

215

short stay of about thirty hours on the quayside, they engaged a car and went to the town, which was an important commercial port and a magnificent city of the French Republic. It was well served by electric trams running from one end to the other and its grand restaurants and other public offices and decorative buildings presented an imposing image. The panoramic view of Marseilles from the great altitude of the sanctuary of *Notre Dame de la Garde* gave a vivid impression of this beautiful city. It had a population of more than 500,000. To enable persons to reach the heights of the *Cathedral Notre Dame* there were lifts constructed on the principle of rope tramcars, called '*Ascenseurs de Notre Dame de la Garde*', for which Dosebai was very grateful!

The passengers from London arrived the next morning and after their embarkation the *Victoria* sailed towards Port Said, where they arrived on the 12th August. Here the ship stopped for the night to pick up the English mail coming from Brindisi. After the arrival of the English mail, they moved further and entered the celebrated Suez Canal, where the speed of the engine was slackened till they moved at walking pace. It took more than thirty hours to pass through the Canal and after calling at Suez, where they did not stop as they used to do before; the *Victoria* steered towards Aden, where they arrived on the morning of 16th August.

When they anchored, there was total chaos with the business of transferring the mailbags and passengers' baggage onto the Bombay boat, which was waiting close by as nearly half the number of passengers were going to India and the others were remaining on the same boat, proceeding to China and Australia. In the midst of it all, coming with his steamboat to escort them ashore, was her old friend, Mr. Hormusji who, with his good-natured wife and all the other members of the family and the whole of their staff, gave them a hearty welcome. They were delighted to meet each other once again in their spacious mansion. Thousands of passengers who had passed through Aden knew the name of Messrs. Cowasji Dinshaw and Brothers. They were the first and foremost in welcoming all the Royals and Viceroys and Governors before they set foot on the shores of India and other Colonies of the East. It was not presumptuous on Dosebai's part to say that the name and the enterprising spirit of the members of her community occupied a front rank among the merchants of the East. Here, in the midst of this lovely company, she and her sons passed half a day, during which they did justice to a sumptuous Parsi dinner in good old Parsi fashion. A friendly reception was not the word for it. Dosebai declared she was accorded a royal reception at the close of her tour.

Taking leave of their host and hostess, they were escorted back to the pier. They went on board the *S.S.Caledonia* where, without any difficulty, they saw all their effects brought from the *S.S. Victoria* and arranged in the cabins. As the passengers were now reduced to half the number, they found the ship very quiet. It was a grand and comfortable boat and they steered to the East in the most delightful weather. Although they were crossing the Indian Ocean in the midst of the monsoon, they escaped the roughest weather and in the company of jovial passengers, days passed like hours. On the morning of 21st August they descried Bombay and soon entered the beautiful harbour, landing on the shores of Bombay hale and hearty after an absence of nearly fifteen months. Joining their friends and relatives with great rejoicing, they drove straight home to their old residence at Tardeo.

The Governor of Bombay, His Excellency Sir George Clarke and his noble wife and daughter had won a high place in the affections of the people of the Bombay Presidency. Dosebai was very sad, therefore, when she heard of the untimely death of Lady Clarke, which plunged the entire Province into mourning. A few months after the lamentable event when her daughter, Miss Constance Violet Clarke, was once more in Bombay, Dosebai wrote to her, expressing a wish to call upon her. She received a reply saying that Miss Clarke would be very pleased to see her. Dosebai, along with her younger son, called on her at Government House. They were given a cordial reception and Miss Clarke impressed them as a highly accomplished and well-informed young lady and a most sympathetic talker. Miss Clarke told Dosebai that she had already heard and read interesting accounts of her adventures, referring especially to the appreciation published by the *Indian Magazine and Review* of August 1908 during Dosebai's last stay in London. She also invited Dosebai to come and have tea with her the following day at the Princess Ladies' Gymkhana. Dosebai expressed her gratitude for the kind thought but had at the same time, to regret her inability to go, as owing to her weak health, she did not feel equal to the task of attending social gatherings.

Hardly ten weeks had elapsed since the interview, when the sudden demise of Miss Clarke herself cast an even deeper gloom than the death of her mother, being such a young woman. During both their lifetimes, mother and daughter had lived and worked amongst the Indians in a manner which may well be followed by other ladies placed in similar positions, offering so much power and opportunity for the discharge of little acts of kindness and sympathy. It was a matter of great satisfaction that Providence had healed the wounds of their universally respected Governor, and the second Lady Clarke was already establishing herself in the hearts of the people, amongst whom she had chosen to cast her social lot.

On the 6th May 1910, the much revered Sovereign, King-Emperor Edward VII, died suddenly of a heart attack. He was loved and mourned by millions and millions of men and women inhabiting His Majesty's worldwide Empire. It was only a few months before this unspeakably sorrowful loss that Dosebai had the unique honour, privilege and pleasure of being presented to the Sovereign and his noble Consort, to whom the hearts of countless loyal subjects went out in spontaneous sympathy. On learning the sad news of the sudden passing away of the great and good Monarch, she telegraphed to Queen Alexandra in London the following message of condolence:

From Mrs. Dosebai Cowasji Jessawalla, Cumballa Hill, Bombay
To
The Private Secretary to Her Majesty Queen Alexandra, London.

Loyal heartfelt condolence from octogenarian Parsi Lady graciously received at Windsor in 1908.
Bewail my lot to bemourn loss of Sovereign.

218

Her humble expression of loyal sympathy on this mournful occasion was acknowledged in the following official reply: -

No.3844
From H.G.Stokes Esq., Deputy Secretary to the Government of India, to Mrs. Dosebai Cowasji Jessawalla, Cumballa Hill, Bombay.

Simla the 7th July 1910
   Home Department (Public)
Madam – I am directed to inform you that the Government of India have received intimation of the receipt of your telegram to the Secretary of State and to express the sincere thanks of the Government of India for the expressions of sympathy and condolence which you have been good enough to convey upon the occasion of the lamented death of His late Majesty the King-Emperor of India.

I have the honour to be, Madam, your most obedient servant,
(Sd.) H.G. Stokes
   Deputy Secretary to the Government of India

CHAPTER 30

CLOSING REFLECTIONS

Here we conclude the stories of Meheribai's and Dosebai's lives, leaving the readers to appreciate what had been accomplished during the half-century and over that they had engaged themselves in the field of women's education and social progress. To enable the generation of the present day to realise the attitude to women that was prevalent at the time when Dosebai became the first Indian girl to go to an English school, amidst the vortex of controversy and opposition, here is an extract from an issue of the Bombay Courier; dated the 19th August 1842: -

"The United Service Gazette of Tuesday stated that a young Parsi lady has been placed as a pupil in Mrs. Ward's seminary, but that the Editor was unable, owing to the lateness of the hour at which the intelligence reached him, to state the father's name; and adds with great truth, 'The Courier will rejoice at it when he knows it.' We consider the man, whose mind is sufficiently enlarged to admit of his taking the initiative in breaking down the prejudices of country and caste, in so good a cause, not only deserving of our humble applause, but of the approbation whish he is sure to obtain of the whole civilized world.

In the East rose the sun of human enlightenment, it travelled westward, and confers that power which consists in knowledge. We of the West are bound, therefore, and feel the obligation to return to its Eastern source, as far as lies in our power, the blessings of enlightenment. The dissemination of knowledge over the whole earth is a paramount object with the philanthropist of every clime. The Parsis, of all the inhabitants of this portion of the globe, ought particularly to appreciate and prize the cultivation of the mental faculties, for to their education is to be attributed in a great degree, if not altogether, their wealth, their liberality and their acknowledged influence. They know this, and they prove their knowledge by the pains they take and the expense they incur, in the education of their male children. Why they have so long neglected their female offspring, can only be accounted for, by their blind subservience to the usage they found established in the country that afforded them protection.

The fear of ridicule, the dislike of innovation have deterred many of even the masterminds of our own country from departing from the established usages of their fatherland, and it required the exercise of the most transcendent moral courage to break the bonds of prejudice and senseless reverence for the time-hallowed and established usage. In considering the sacrifice which this Parsee gentleman has made, of early prejudice, we do not regard it as an occurrence of ephemeral interest, but as a type and forerunner of superior intellectual advancement amongst the class to which he belongs; and we hail it as a happy omen of what may be accomplished even in our own day. "

The *Courier,* however, made a serious mistake in one respect, which it was most essential to rectify. It mentioned that Dosebai was educated by her father. This was completely erroneous, as at the time Dosebai started going to school, her father was not even alive as he had died four years earlier. Thus her mother alone was her sole guardian and as such, evinced great care and solicitude in looking after Dosibai. It was a very courageous step that she took in placing her daughter in Mrs. Ward's English Seminary at the tender age of ten. For this, the credit belonged solely to her late revered mother, Bai Meheribai, and in justice to her memory Dosebai rectified this error of the *Courier* even at such a remote date as 70 years after the event.

Dosebai lived to see great changes in the status of women, not only amongst the Parsi community, but also around the world. She died on the 11th January 1911, just six years before the women of England got the power to vote. She would have been well pleased with the powerful women of our present generation – who knows, she might even have made a great President!

THE   END